Great Leaps

Phonological Awareness

and

Language Development

Activities

for the

Emergent Reader

Kenneth U. Campbell

Gainesville, Florida

Diarmuid, Inc.

© 2013

Phonological Awareness and Language Development Activities for the Emergent Reader:

GREAT LEAPS

Diarmuid, Inc.

To Cecil Mercer

- *you inspired a generation of special teachers*

- *you were the most special of all*

- *the world is better because of you*

- *thank-you*

Phonological Awareness and Language Development Activities for the Emergent Reader

Kenneth U. Campbell

Great Leaps

Diarmuid, Inc.

Gainesville, FL 32635

Copyright © 2013 by Kenneth U. Campbell. All rights reserved.

ISBN Number: 978-1-59347-000-5

No forms of this book or parts of this book may be reproduced or utilized in any form or by any means electronic or mechanical, including photocopying, recording or by any information storage and retrieval system, without the expressed written consent of the author.

Published by *Diarmuid, Inc.*
www.greatleaps.com

Table of Contents

Preface xix

Acknowledgements xxi

About the Author xxiii

Introduction xxv

Section I. Word and Sentence Awareness

       Eliciting and Building Language Experience 2

Lesson 1.	Simple Word Repeating 6	
	Expressive Language Preparation 7	
	Oral Expression 9	
	Building Vocabulary – the Bear 10	
	Singing – *Hey Mickey* 11	
Lesson 2.	Simple Word Repeating 12	
	Oral Expression 13	
	Building Vocabulary – the Elephant 14	
	Singing – *Where are You Tonight* 15	
Lesson 3.	Simple Word Repeating 16	
	Oral Expression 17	
	Building Vocabulary – the Crow 18	
	Singing – *Mommy Loves Me* 19	
Lesson 4.	Simple Pseudo-word Repeating 22	
	Oral Expression 23	
	Building Vocabulary – the Snake 24	
	Games - Mother May I, Simon Says 25	

	Singing – *Hit the Road Jack*	27
Lesson 5.	Simple Sentence Repeating	30
	Expressive Language	31
	Building Vocabulary – the Dolphin	32
	Singing – *Have You Ever Seen a Lassie*	33
Lesson 6.	Simple Sentence Repeating	34
	Expressive Language	35
	Building Vocabulary – the Rabbit	36
	Singing – *My Bonnie*	37
Lesson 7.	Sentence Repeating	39
	Expressive Language	40
	Building Vocabulary – the Tiger	41
	Singing – *For He's a Jolly Good Fellow*	42
Lesson 8.	Repeating Sentences	43
	Expressive Language	44
	Building Vocabulary – the Butterfly	45
	Singing – *Skinny Marink (Skidda Marink)*	46
Lesson 9.	Tapping Words	48
	Expressive Language	49
	Building Vocabulary – the Kangaroo	50
	Singing – *The Itsy Bitsy Spider*	51
Lesson 10.	Sentence Repeating	52
	Expressive Language	53
	Building Vocabulary – the Shark	54
	Singing – *My Hand on My Head*	55
Lesson 11.	Tapping Words	56
	Expressive Language	57

	Building Vocabulary – the Monkey	58
	Singing – *Brother John*	59
Lesson 12.	Making Words from Syllables	61
	Expressive Language	62
	Building Vocabulary – the Cow	63
	Singing – *One, Two Buckle My Shoe*	64
Lesson 13.	Breaking Words into Syllables	65
	Expressive Language	66
	Building Vocabulary – Milk	67
	Singing – *Hokey Pokey*	68

Section II. Building Words, Sentences and Vocabulary

Lesson 14.	Forming Words then Sentences	73
	Expression Language	74
	Building Vocabulary – Peanut Butter	75
	Singing – *Around the Mulberry Bush*	76
Lesson 15.	Defining Words	78
	Expression Language	79
	Building Vocabulary – Potatoes	80
	Game – Potatoes	81
	Singing – *Shoo Fly*	82
Lesson 16.	Vocabulary Building	83
	Expression Language	84
	Building Vocabulary – Apples	85
	Singing – *Joy to the World*	86
Lesson 17.	Vocabulary Building	87

	Expression Language	88
	Building Vocabulary – Cereal	89
	Singing – *The Bear Went Over the Mountain*	90
Lesson 18.	Vocabulary Building	91
	Expression Language	92
	Building Vocabulary – Broccoli	93
	Singing – *Dem Bones*	94
Lesson 19.	Turning Phrases into Sentences	95
	Expressive Language	96
	Building Vocabulary – Carrots	97
	Singing – *The Little Green Frog*	98
Lesson 20.	Turning Phrases into Sentences	99
	Expression Language	100
	Building Vocabulary – Tomatoes	101
	Singing – *If You're Happy and You Know It*	102

Section III. Rhyming 103

Lesson 21.	Rhyming	106
	Building Vocabulary – Onions	107
Lesson 22.	Rhyming	108
	Expressive Language	109
	Building Vocabulary – Bread	110
	Singing – *I'm a Little Teapot*	111
Lesson 23.	Rhyming	112
	Expressive Language	113

	Singing – *Hey, Ho, Nobody Home*	115
Lesson 24.	Rhyming	116
	Singing – *Take Me Out to the Ballgame*	117
Lesson 25.	Rhyming	118
	Singing – *I'm Henery the Eighth, I Am*	119
Lesson 26.	Rhyming	120
	Singing – *Knick Knack*	121
Lesson 27.	Rhyming	122
	Singing – *Miss Mary Mack*	123
Lesson 28.	Rhyming	124
	Singing – *It's Raining, It's Pouring*	125
Lesson 29.	Rhyming	126
	Singing – *Pop Goes the Weasel*	127
Lesson 30.	Rhyming	128
	Singing – *Over the River and Through the Woods*	129
Lesson 31.	Rhyming	130
	Singing – *Cinderella Dressed in Yella*	131
Lesson 32.	Rhyming	132
	Singing – *The Ants Go Marching*	133

Section IV. Phonemic Awareness 135

Lesson 33.	Beginning Sounds	138
	Singing – *I've Been Working on the Railroad*	139
Lesson 34.	Ending Sounds	140
	Singing – *If I Had a Hammer*	141
Lesson 35.	Beginning Sounds	142

	Singing – *A Sailor Went to Sea, Sea, Sea* 143
Lesson 36.	Beginning Sounds 144
	Singing – *Tiny Tim the Turtle* 145
Lesson 37.	Alliteration 146
	Singing – *Billy Goat Hide and Seek* 147
Lesson 38.	Alliteration 148
	Singing – *Engine, Engine Number Nine* 149
Lesson 39.	Consonant Blends 150
	Singing – *Suwanee River* 151
Lesson 40.	Ending Sounds 152
	Singing – *She Threw it Out the Window* 153
Lesson 41.	Using Contextual Clues 154
	Singing – *The Muffin Man* 155
Lesson 42.	Beginning Sounds 156
	Singing – *Yankee Doodle* 157
Lesson 43.	Beginning Sounds 158
	Singing – *John Jacob Jingleheimer Schmidt* 159
Lesson 44.	Beginning Sounds 160
	Singing – *The Grand Old Duke of York* 161
Lesson 45.	Beginning Sounds 162
	Singing – *This Little Light of Mine* 163
Lesson 46.	Ending Sounds 164
	Singing – *Little Liza Jane* 165
Lesson 47.	Blends 166
	Singing – *Clementine* 167
Lesson 48.	Ending Sounds 168
	Singing – *When Johnny Comes Marching Home* 169

Lesson 49.	Blends	170
	Singing – *Ten in the Bed*	171
Lesson 50.	Vowel Sounds	172
	Singing – *Aiken Drum*	173
Lesson 51.	Vowel Sounds	174
	Singing – *Crawdad Hole*	175
Lesson 52.	Beginning Sounds	176
	Singing – *Down By the Riverside*	177
Lesson 53.	Ending Sounds	178
	Activity – Last Names.	179
Lesson 54.	Vowel Sounds	180
	Singing - *Apples and Bananas*	181

Section V. Morphological Awareness & Language Acuity ... 183

Lesson 55.	Verb Tense	186
Lesson 56.	Verb Tense	187
Lesson 57.	Verb Tense	188
Lesson 58.	Verb Tense	189
Lesson 59.	Verb Tense	190
Lesson 60.	Plurals	191
	Singing – *There's a Hole*	192
Lesson 61.	Plurals	193
Lesson 62.	Plurals	194
	Song – *Flying Purple People Eater*	195
Lesson 63.	Plural to Singular	196

	Singing – *There Was an Old Lady Who Swallowed a Fly*	197
Lesson 64.	Ordinal Numbers	198
	Expressive Language Development	199
Lesson 65.	Language Facility – Plurals and Verb Tense	200
Lesson 66.	Working with Affixes	202
Lesson 67.	Prefixes	203
Lesson 68.	Prefixes	204
Lesson 69.	Prefixes	205
Lesson 70.	Prefixes	206
Lesson 71.	Prefixes	207
Lesson 72.	Suffixes – *ing*	208
Lesson 73.	Suffixes – *er*	209
	Singing – *Kookaburra*	210
Lesson 74.	Suffixes - *-tion* and *–sion*	211
Lesson 75.	Suffixes – *ician*	212
Lesson 76.	Suffixes – Comparatives – Superlatives	214
Lesson 77.	Reversals	215
	Preparing to Work with Spoonerisms	216
Lesson 78.	Spoonerisms – Food	217
Lesson 79.	Spoonerisms – Creatures	218
Lesson 80.	Spoonerisms – Things	219
Lesson 81.	Spoonerisms – Places	220
Lesson 82.	Spoonerisms - Sentences	221
Lesson 83.	Language Acuity	222
Lesson 84.	Language Acuity	223
Lesson 85.	Language Acuity	224
Lesson 86.	Language Acuity	225

Lesson 87.	**Logic – Conditionals**	226
	Singing – *Oh Susannah*	227
Appendix		229
	Scope and Sequence	231
	Song List	233
	RTI	234
	Progress Charts	236
	Glossary	240

Preface

As I travel the country with *Great Leaps*, I hear a recurring theme. Students do not comprehend what they read beyond the third grade level. Seemingly, educational tactics to this point are failing to break down this third grade comprehension wall. At a conference sponsored by the New York Branch of the International Dyslexia Association, I heard Dr. Carmen Farina, the deputy chancellor for teaching and learning with the New York City public schools, address this very problem in her keynote speech. She identified the problem as the result of language deficits in the children. At the same time, I was reading Betty Hart and Tod Risley's 30-million word gap study in their seminal research book *Meaningful Differences in the Everyday Experience of Young American Children*. I then knew our work had to go beyond teaching children and giving them experience with reading comprehension tactics. I knew that we had to attack language skill development. This begins with phonological awareness.

I spent the next two years studying the language patterns of children of poverty from Howard Middle and Fessenden Elementary Schools of Marion County in North Central Florida. I listened to the children talk and recorded much of what I heard. I then did Fry readabilities on their language and found it alarmingly deficient. In the case of many of the middle school students, their expressive language did not even meet their very basic social needs, much less the academic requirements.

With this knowledge, I then studied and designed interventions to attack these language inadequacies in common sense daily activities. Next, I worked with colleagues and professionals to brainstorm, evaluate and then organize my work so that it could be included in our three major *Great Leaps Reading* fluency programs.

I know the single most important determinant for the success of a student in reading is not only their facility with language, but also their background in phonological awareness. The earlier we begin these lessons in life, the better the prognosis or outcome. Included in these interventions will be phonemic awareness, morphemic awareness, and language development activities. These preparatory activities will go a long way toward strengthening and improving our children's reading and comprehension development.

These lessons in phonological awareness and language development need to be a part of a young child's daily routine. The results from these exercises will serve to make a significant difference in our children's reading abilities.

Acknowledgements

Cecil Mercer
> *Professor Emeritus in Special Education – University of Florida - retired*

Luz Font
> *Professor of Spanish – Florida State College*

Diana Campbell
> *Editing and Team Member – Great Leaps*

Patricia Campbell
> *Editor – Jacksonville, Florida*

Melody Ritchie
> *Editing and Team Member – Great Leaps*

Mike Boehlein
> *Fine Images – Gainesville, Florida*

About the Author

Kenneth U. Campbell

Kenneth U. Campbell is a retired educator with thirty years of teaching experience in the field of special education. He is a graduate of the University of Florida and holds a Florida teaching certification in language arts, social studies, behavior disorders and learning disabilities. In his extensive career, Mr. Campbell has taught children of all ages, from four years old in pre-school to young adults in high school, as well as non-readers in prison. He spent years teaching as an adjunct professor for Florida Southern College of Orlando teaching recertification classes in behavior disorders and learning disabilities.

Kenneth Campbell is the author of *Great Leaps*, a reading fluency program currently in use in thousands of schools throughout the United States and Canada, and in forty other countries around the world. He has dedicated his life to the teaching of children with learning difficulties, especially in reading and math. He is a frequent presenter at national conferences and spends much of his time training educators on the art of teaching reading to children reading at below grade level.

Mr. Campbell has received many awards, including the prestigious 2011 Landis Stetler Award for Educational Leadership from the Council for Exceptional Children in the state of Florida. Kenneth Campbell has also been elected as the President of Florida's Council for Children with Behavior Disorders, has served as a Board member of several educational associations and Officer of the Florida Education Association. He is an active member of the Council for Exceptional Children, the Learning Disabilities Association, the International Dyslexia Association and Everyone Reading.

Introduction

Virtually every child can be taught to read. With proper leadership, heart and commitment we know our children can be taught to read fluently with comprehension. The long history of reading failure in our country can be easily turned around. The best way to begin these significant changes is by ensuring each young child has adequate preparation in phonological awareness and has had considerable, meaningful language development. We need the leadership to implement affordable interventions. We need the will of the country and its heart to demand that all children be taught to their potential. We need the commitment of educators to demand and follow through with programs that meet the needs of all of our children, no exceptions.

Proficiency in sound and language awareness significantly improves a young child's reading prognosis. Experts, especially in neuro-science, strongly support the idea that work in phonological awareness can productively begin between ages three and four. Some children can begin this work at early age three and some are not ready until after their 4th birthday. Most children in the United States get this preparation naturally at home. Progress can be accelerated with the proper materials.

The best readiness assessment involves the child's expressive language abilities. Our work in phonological awareness can begin as early as the child can speak independently in coherent sentences. It should continue one step at a time until mastery; there is no hurry. Mastery is the ability to proficiently do a lesson in one minute or less independently without error. When a lesson is mastered, it is then time to introduce and begin working on the next lesson. Mastery can take from one day to ten or so days. If the tasks in these materials are laborious and become a daily struggle for the child or children, the implementation plans need to be reassessed. Several of the lessons in the final section are quite challenging with very high expectations. There may be children who will find the activities frustrating or impossible. Not every child will be able to successfully complete the final section before age seven.

The first lessons involve words, syllables and sentences. Supplementing this work will be activities in language, verbal thought and expression and singing. These are all considered essentials in early childhood development for emergent readers. The work in this program can be done effectively in small groups or individually.

The instructor must be well-versed in the materials, knowing when to seamlessly enter these activities into the classroom day. These interventions must never be a substitute for a preferred activity, that is, students must not be sent for remediation during a highly preferred activity such as physical education, music or art. Interruptions must be kept to a minimum. The program should be scheduled for every day of the week. With the purchase of a book of their own, parents can also get involved in these interventions, to even better the student's awareness and facility with word and syllabic awareness. These are the very foundations of phonological awareness. To further help increase later reading comprehension, considerable work in language acquisition and utilization are included.

Lessons include numerous instructional tips as well as background information and rationale when relevant.

The lessons work within the fifteen-minute or so attention span limits of young children. The daily activities conclude with singing, which involves the entire brain working with the child's language centers. Music is an essential part of all human expression. Like speech, it appears to arise naturally in all cultures. When music is combined with language and activities, much is gained. A singing group is generally a happy group.

Our music selections need no songbook nor musical instruments. Of course, adding a variety of musical instruments would only enhance the activity. The music should not be omitted because there are no instruments available. These activities are an essential part in building phonological awareness and language development.

The tune for each of the songs in this book can be easily found by looking up the name of the song in your search engine. Many of these online videos also include variations of the song and a variety of activities that can be done during the singing. The leader of the singing should lead in a loud, happy voice filled with appropriate expression; this is no time to be shy or to worry about what outsiders looking in may think of you. You should not be self-conscious about performing with and for your little ones. Have that "itsy, bitsy spider" climb. Row that boat, even not so gently down the stream. Show the class a "knick knack paddy whack! and give that dog a bone." Having a good time is pleasantly contagious.

The songs do not have to be done in the order presented, nor do all the songs have to be sung. Additions are also appropriate, especially the addition of seasonal or regional favorites. The activities of the songs can be amended or expanded to meet the needs and abilities of the students.

As the children build up a repertoire of songs, more time can be allocated for singing. Eventually, the children should be able to request a song or lead the group in one of their favorite songs or activities. These early chances of leadership will enhance the likelihood of their future performance in group activities.

Music is essential in early childhood education. It should be an everyday part of the school day. Know that via music, song and dance, we build up student language abilities and confidence.

Section I

Word

and

Sentence Awareness

Section I

Word and Sentence Awareness

The first activities involve phonological awareness are in simple word and sentence repeating. Repeating simple words is used to teach a child the concept of a word as well as assess the child's very short-term memory. We are also stimulating the proper areas of the brain for the eventual movement into reading. This lesson may seem of the utmost simplicity, but be assured it is a critical step in phonological awareness. It is important that the child leaves each lesson knowing that we are talking about words.

The instructor of a small group for the word and sentence repeating activities must have their book turned to the correct page with a countdown timer set to one minute. As a lesson progresses, the instructor must be prepared to move about the class observing student performance, and if necessary taking notes, mental or written, as the very short lesson proceeds. The children need to be carefully trained from the beginning in how to give a proper response. In this activity, the instructor will say the word, then the child or the children will repeat the word exactly as spoken.

The tutor of a single child or a group of two or three needs to sit across from the child or group. The countdown timer must be set to one-minute and the child or children calm and ready to proceed. Everyone should be very comfortable and relaxed. If per chance the timer and being timed is perceived as threatening or as too much pressure, use a countdown timer that has a light to let the tutor know when the one-minute is up. Timers can be purchased at greatleaps.com. Please be aware that most often, the fear of being timed is an adult-induced behavior; there is nothing inherently threatening about the use of a timer. When timing these exercises, an exact minute is not absolutely essential. Five to ten seconds over will have little or no negative impact on the activity.

When the tutor reads a word, it must be read slowly with proper care taken for pronunciation and even intonation. An example of the lesson will be given so the child or children will know what to do and how to respond. If one example does not suffice, do two or even three. The main focus needs to be on student performance and achievement. When reading slowly, the instructor must continue to properly intonate after the response giving immediate feedback, either, praising the successful effort or correcting the student response. Immediate and focused correction is powerful.

Eliciting and Building Language Experience

These exercises are designed to build up a child's verbal repertoire. Daily work, thinking and practice will significantly enhance the child's verbal and receptive language acumen. The younger the student, the better the student's brain plasticity for learning new things and acquiring language; thus, the more significant the impact of coordinated daily work and activities.

The instructor presents the word of the lesson to the student or group. Students with language difficulties will need to be gently led into broadening their abilities to build upon the presented theme or idea. Some children will work for the first few months of this program at the very concrete or simplistic level with difficulty in language abstraction. Each child is different and each child develops individually. Children who have not had the benefit of living in a rich language environment or children who have missed considerable language due to hearing problems will most likely lag behind their peers. These lessons are all the more important for them. We know that the earlier the work in phonological awareness, the better the impact on reading and writing.

In working the *Developing Expressive Language Activities*, it is the mission of the instructor to elicit higher-level thinking through thought out questioning, commenting and reinforcing the responses and responders.

The following is an example of what a lesson may sound like if a small group of children have been asked to talk about the word *house*.

Instructor: What do you know about the word "house"?

Student I: I live in a house.

Instructor: Yes, can anyone else tell me something about a house?

Student 2: Mine is green.

Instructor: Yes, Becky. I like the way your hand is raised and you are waiting on me to call on you.

Becky. I don't live in a house, I live in an apartment.

Instructor: Yes, not everyone lives in a house. A lot of us live in apartments.

Student 1: Houses got windows and doors.

Instructor: Yes

Becky: They have roofs! So do apartments!

Instructor: Yes, houses and apartments have roofs.

Student 3: Birds walk on roofs.

(Now the topic is moving away and needs redirection.)

Instructor: *Besides roofs, doors and windows, what else do houses have?*

Student 1: They have yards.

Instructor: Yes, some houses have big yards with them and some very little.

Becky: Mine doesn't have a yard at all. We have to go to the playground.

Student 2: Houses have rooms!

Student 4: They have kitchens and bathrooms.

Instructor: Anyone else want to tell us something they know about houses?

Student 3: And bedrooms.

Becky: Some houses have pianos in them.

Instructor: Good, good.

Instructor: Anything else?

Student 1: My house has a fireplace.

The lesson only needs to last until you see a slowdown in the responses or children getting off task to the point of no return. These talks should only take a few minutes. If a great discussion arises, go with it, allowing every participant to take part. We grow in language by thinking and using it.

Instructor: Yesterday, we talked about houses.

Instructor: Can anyone remember and tell me some of the things that houses have?

(The instructor looks around approving the efforts.). I like the way you are quietly raising your hands and waiting for me to call on you! Jamie?

Jamie: Some of them had roofs, and a fireplace, and yards!

Instructor: Good job, Jamie!

Becky: They are a lot like apartments because people live in them. They all have doors and windows.

Jamie: They have roofs and steps.

Instructor: Don't forget to raise your hand. I'll call on you. What can you think of that we didn't mention yesterday?

Student 1: Houses can have cars in front of them.

Instructor: Yes. Jamie, I saw you raise that hand for me.

Jamie: They can have television sets in them.

And so forth. The leader of the activity must maintain the rules and reinforce the desired behaviors. Call on a variety of students. Make relevant comments to keep the discussion moving or take it into more depth. The key is maintaining on task behavior while guiding the lesson so that all can take part. Attention is necessary for there to be the vocabulary development we desire. The instructor must also be able to keep up and manage the conversation, so that opportunities for more in depth discussion with higher vocabulary can be gained.

Simple Word Repeating

Preparing for Lesson 1

The instructor is going to say, *"I am going to say a word. I want you to repeat the word to me exactly as I say it to you. Let's try one for practice."* These instructions are not an absolute script, it is most important that the student understands exactly what he/she is expected to do for the lesson to be successful. The timing of the actual activity should not begin until the instructor is assured everyone participating can follow the directions, comfortable and ready to proceed.

The instructor says, *"pizza."* The individual or group should repeat the word exactly as it has been presented. The instructor of a group should be moving around the classroom and carefully listening to student responses so as to ascertain those having any difficulties or not participating. Encouragement and coaching are encouraged.

When she feels assured that everyone can take part, she says, *"Now, we'll begin. Remember, repeat the word exactly like I read it to you."*

The instructor sets the countdown timer for 30 seconds and begins. If the exercise is completed correctly in thirty seconds and there are no difficulties within the group, it is mastered. When a lesson has been mastered, on the next day of instruction you will proceed to the next lesson. Each word not correctly repeated is an error. In working with individuals, when a student completes an exercise in one minute or less, a goal *–leap* -- has been accomplished. Group work must often be handled differently; the activity will be repeated daily until the instructor is certain that every student capable of mastering the lesson has done so. When a goal has been made, the student(s) will begin on the next day to work on Lesson 2. Some lessons need only take one day, other lessons may require up to a week. Lessons should not require more than one week. Errors are immediately corrected and if necessary, remediated by a short lesson or practice after the timed exercise.

Simple Word Repeating

Lesson 1

Timed Activity (30 seconds)

Instructor: *"I am going to say a word. I want you to repeat the word to me exactly as I say it to you. Let's try one for practice."* The instructor says, *"Pizza."*

The class or student repeats the word in unison. When everyone understands the directions, it is time for the timed lesson. If there is any student confusion choose another practice word.

Instructor: *"Okay, now we're ready to start. Begin."* (the timer is started)

1. monkey
2. car
3. banana
4. smell
5. store
6. singing
7. football
8. puppy
9. lollipop
10. wind
11. water
12. swim
13. throw
14. laugh
15. driving

Developing Expressive Language

Preparing for Activity 1

The instructor will read a word from the lesson, then ask questions or make comments intended to lead to a discussion. It is then the task of the instructor to lead a short group discussion. The objective is to increase student thinking and to increase the depth of response. When excitement is generated, the job of the instructor is considerably easier. When appropriate, the instructor should encourage elaboration. The instructor can also paraphrase student response with a higher level of vocabulary. If there is no student interest in the activity, move on to the next discussion question. There is no need in the program to ask all the questions. The objective is to get the students talking and thinking about their responses and what to say next.

It is important that the instructor chooses who is to answer a question. It is also important that everyone take part. It is a good practice to choose the quieter or "lower" student to give the first response. Otherwise, the child may not be getting the opportunity to think out responses and thus develop the intended skills. Brighter students will most likely be developing their own response based on the initial question as well as the responses that have followed. Thus, everyone is being encouraged to develop neural thinking skills. A student or two cannot be allowed to dominate the classroom environment. If there is any personal dominating going on, it should be from the instructor.

Example:

Instructor: "June, I just love the way you are sitting."

Then the instructor asks June the question because she was the one following the directions. If when you praise June, you notice little Mac suddenly moving to sit perfectly, it would be very reinforcing to note that as it happens and call on Mac next.

Example:

Instructor: Can anyone in the room swim? (June's hand is the only one up.)

Instructor: I see that June has her hand up. June?

June: I don't like water in my eyes.

Instructor: I don't like water in my eyes either. When I was your age, I wore goggles to keep the water out of my eyes. Then one day, I found out it didn't bother me anymore.

Instructor: (There are no hands raised.) Mac: Can you swim?

Mac: No.

If the question does not generate conversation, move to another. Pursue and reinforce student responses.

Before an activity is completed, all students should be given the chance to respond, especially the introverts. It is very worthwhile that the instructor controls the response activity. She may call on those who have not raised their hands. Those with language problems or those needing the most language development should be given first opportunity to respond to most of these activities. This will encourage them to develop thought-response behavior rather than building upon the thoughts and the responses of the other, more adept students. Of course the child with the advanced skills is eager to show off. It is the job of the instructor to manage that eagerness so that all students will have an opportunity to grow. This can never be done with nagging or punishment, no matter how subtle. The best and most lasting gains are accomplished through efficient and fair management of the group.

The purpose of these language enhancement activities is to generate and stimulate student thinking. This is often silent observable behavior. You can watch a student taking the ideas and thinking as he forms ideas into words. This will take longer for some students than others. Thus, it is important that children be given adequate time to process and then respond. In a world dominated by extroverts, many children are left out of the discussion. It will take instructor leadership and manipulation to insure that each student will have the opportunity to make gains from these activities. Instructors also tend to spend too much time themselves in directing the activity. Gentle coordination and direction will often lead to the most exciting conversational gains. The instructor is more like the conductor of an orchestra rather than the maestro performer. When a conversation amongst the class really begins moving, the classroom and the rapport gained make teaching an absolute pleasure.

Developing Expressive Language

Activity 1

Oral Expression

This activity is untimed. It is left up to instructor discretion how far to pursue a given conversation. Remember, take the ball and run with it. If the question goes nowhere, move on to the next. These do not all have to be covered. Choose the question you believe will give you the best conversational encounter.

1. Besides a monkey, what other animals can you see at the zoo? Are all the animals in cages? Do some animals visit the zoo?

2. Why do we have cars? Do your parents have a car? What kind of car would you like to have?

3. Why don't people dip their bananas in catsup like they do with French fries? What would taste good with a banana?

4. What is the best smell you can think of? Which smells better, cupcakes baking or popcorn?

5. Where do people buy clothes? What kinds of clothes can you think of?

6. Where do people sing? Do you like to sing? What is your favorite song?

7. How is a football different from a basketball?

8. What do puppies do? What do kittens do?

9. What is your favorite color of lollipop? Why do lollipops have color?

10. Where does the wind come from? Where does it go?

11. What does water taste like? What does orange juice taste like?

12. When is the best time to go swimming?

13. What are some things you can throw? What is something that you could not throw?

14. Laugh without making a noise.

15. What are some things that people can drive? What is the biggest thing you can think of that has wheels?

Building Vocabulary

Preparing for Lesson 1

Bear

Instructor: *I am going to tell you the name of an animal. I want you to think of this animal for a little while and then raise your hand to give me a word or two to tell me something you know about it. It can be the color, what the animal looks like, where you can find them, their size and anything else about that animal you can think of. Let's do a practice one first. If I said 'wolf', what would you think of?*

The instructor calls on students who have raised their hands. The students give a variety of responses.

Instructor *Yes, they can be scary (taking time to clearly enunciate between the words) big   bad   sharp teeth   killers   run fast   they howl Good job! Our first word in building up our vocabularies is – **bear.***

What color is a bear?

What kinds of bears are there?

What do bears eat?

Where do bears live?

Do you know any stories about bears?

Note: You can have the students draw a picture of a bear doing something. Students then may stand at their desk or seat and show their picture and describe what they wrote. From their first days in a school setting students should get used to the expectation of describing their work or talking with the group.

Developing Expressive Language

Singing

Hey Mickey!

This song can be used to help let everyone in the class get to know each other's names. From Mickey you could go to *Hey! Sharika: Sharika, Sharika, you're so fine...* for instance: *"Hey, fried chicken – chicken, chicken you're so fine... Hey donuts..."*

"Hey Mickey" © Toni Basil

Use your search engine to look up Toni Basil's "Hey Mickey!" Make sure to practice and have the tune down to a tee before working with the children.

Simple Word Repeating

Lesson 2

Timed Activity (30 seconds)

Instructor: *"I am going to say a word. I want you to repeat the word to me exactly as I say it to you. Let's try one for practice."* The instructor says, *"Pizza."*

The class or student repeats the word in unison. When everyone understands the directions, it is time for the timed lesson. If there is any student confusion have another practice word.

Instructor*: "Okay, now we're ready to start. Begin."*

1. bobcat
2. truck
3. jump
4. sleep
5. barracuda
6. violin
7. airplane
8. kitten
9. clock
10. thunder
11. juice
12. cloud
13. hurricane
14. smiling
15. purple

Developing Expressive Language

Activity 2

Oral Expression

This activity is untimed. It is left up to instructor discretion how far to pursue a given conversation. Remember, take the ball and run with it. If the question goes nowhere, move on to the next. They do not all have to be covered. Choose the most interesting ones for your student or group.

1. A bobcat is a large, wild cat that lives in the woods or forest. Name some other cats larger than a housecat.

2. Why do we have trucks? Do you know anyone who has a truck? What kind of truck is it? Name one kind of truck.

3. When are some times and places you like to jump?

4. Why do you think people have to sleep?

5. A barracuda is a rather large fish with very sharp teeth. What other animals live in the oceans and rivers?

6. A violin is a musical instrument that is played in an orchestra. Name some other musical instruments.

7. How is an airplane different from a car? How are they alike?

8. What is a kitten? What colors can they be?

9. What is the purpose of a clock? Why do we need them?

10. Are you afraid of thunder? Why?

11. What is your favorite juice?

12. What is a cloud? What kinds of different clouds have you seen? Are there clouds outside now?

13. Tell me what you know about hurricanes.

14. Let me look around and see who is smiling. What are some things that can make you smile?

15. Look around and tell me if there is anything purple in the room.

Building Vocabulary

Lesson 2

Elephant

Instructor: *I am going to tell you the name of an animal. I want you to think of this animal for a little while and then raise your hand to give me a word or two to tell me something you know about it. It can be the color, what the animal looks like, where you can find them, their size and anything else about that animal you can think of. Let's do a practice one first.*

Last time we spoke about bears. Today, we'll talk about an animal much larger. Name an animal larger than a bear. Today, we'll think and talk about elephants. Tell me something you know about elephants.

What color is an elephant?

What do elephants eat?

Where do elephants live?

Do you know any stories about elephants?

Note: You can have the students draw a picture of an elephant doing something. Students then may stand at their desk or seat and show their picture and describe what they wrote. From their first days in a school setting students should get used to the expectation of describing their work or talking with the group.

Developing Expressive Language

Singing

Where Are You Tonight
©1952 Susan Heather

This song was a favorite of many years ago on the country music show, *Hee Haw*. Buck Owens and Roy Clark adapted the 1952 song of Susan Heather for the show.

Get the words and tune from your search engine. You can watch it being performed on the original show. With permission, you can show the song to the class and they can sing along. You can substitute the names of the children in the class for the word 'you' as in "Where, where is Charlie tonight?"

This activity can help children get to know each other's names early in the school year.

Simple Word Repeating

Lesson 3

Timed Activity (30 seconds)

Instructor: *"I am going to say a word. Then, I want you to repeat the word to me exactly as I have said it to you. Let's try one for practice.*

camel ...

"Okay, now we're ready to start. Begin."

1. elephant
2. parachute
3. table
4. finger
5. toe
6. guitar
7. grass
8. cucumber
9. frown
10. circus
11. mall
12. party
13. stick
14. doctor
15. haircut

Developing Expressive Language

Activity 3

Oral Expression

This activity is untimed. It is left up to instructor discretion how far to pursue a given conversation. Remember, take the ball and run with it. If the question goes nowhere, move on to the next. They do not all have to be covered.

1. Describe an elephant to me.
2. A parachute is made of cloth and strings. If you have a parachute you can jump from an airplane and go slowly down. If you were high in the sky coming down in a parachute, what are some things you would look down to see?
3. What are some things you see on a table?
4. Show me one of your fingers. What are the names of our five fingers?
5. How are toes like fingers? How are they different?
6. Who do you know that can play a guitar?
7. What kinds of games can you play on a nice grass field?
8. A cucumber is a green vegetable that is used to make pickles. Name some other vegetables.
9. Everyone frown and make me a sad face. What can make you frown?
10. I heard the circus is coming to town. What will I see there?
11. What are some things I can buy at the mall? What are some things I can do at the mall?
12. What are some things you like about parties?
13. I found a long stick in the park. What are some things I could do with it?
14. What is the job of a doctor?
15. I need a haircut. Where should I go?

Building Vocabulary

Preparing for Lesson 3

Crow

Instructor: *I am going to tell you the name of a kind of bird. I want you to think of this bird for a little while and then raise your hand to give me a word or two to tell me something you know about it. It can be the color, what the bird looks like, where you can find them, their size and anything else about that bird you can think of. Let's do a practice one first.*

What color is a crow?

What sound do they make?

What kind of trouble do they get in?

Where do crows live?

Do you know any stories about crows?

Note: You can have the students draw a picture of a crow doing something. Students then may stand at their desk or seat and show their picture and describe what they wrote

Developing Expressive Language

Singing

Mommy Loves Me

Mommy loves me, this I know
Because I heard her tell me so.
We are family, I belong.
I am weak but she is strong,

Yes, Mommy loves me.
Yes, Mommy loves me.
Yes, Mommy loves me.
I heard her tell me so.

Daddy loves me, this I know ..
My Grandma loves me, this I know …
My Grandpa loves me, this I know …

Tune "Jesus Loves Me" by William Batchelder Bradbury, 1862. Original Words by Anna Bartlett Warner adapted by Kenneth U. Campbell 2013.

Preparing for Lesson 4
Simple Pseudo-word Repeating

In this exercise, students will be asked to repeat nonsense syllables or nonsense words. One of the secrets of the success of *Great Leaps* is that complex ideas have been organized simply so that what we have learned from the science can now be easily and affordably utilized for student progress. Though the exercise may appear novel, it is very helpful in the development of student phonological awareness.

When someone encounters a word they do not know, they often search "their brain" and use every clue possible to see if they can determine what the word means. That search involves considerable neural activity. The activity is what we seek, not the creativity of the response. The search is enough.

*****

The instructor is going to say, *"I am going to say what sounds like a word. It is a made up word. I want you to repeat it to me exactly as I say it to you. Let's try one for practice."* These instructions are not an absolute script. It is most important that the student understand exactly what he/she is expected to do for the lesson to be successful. It is important to speak clearly and naturally to your student or class. If the directions need to be simplified, do it.

The timing of the actual activity should not begin until the instructor is assured everyone participating can follow the directions, is comfortable and ready to proceed.

When instructor says, *"woff,"* the individual or group should repeat the word exactly as it has been presented. The instructor of a group should be constantly moving around the classroom, carefully listening to student responses so as to ascertain those having any difficulties or not participating. Encouragement and coaching are encouraged.

The instructor, *"Now, we'll begin. Remember, repeat this made up word exactly like I read it to you."*

The instructor sets the countdown timer and begins. If the exercise is completed correctly in less than one minute and there are no difficulties within the group, it is mastered. When a lesson has been mastered, on the next day of instruction you will proceed to the next lesson. Each word not correctly repeated is an error. In working with individuals, when a student completes an exercise in one minute or less, a goal –*leap* -- has been accomplished.

Group work must often be handled differently; the activity will be repeated daily until the instructor is certain that every student capable of mastering the lesson has indeed done so. When a goal has been made, the student(s) will begin on the next day to work on the next lesson. Some lessons need only take one day, other lessons may require up to a week. Errors are immediately corrected and, if felt necessary, remediated by a short lesson or practice after the timed exercise.

Simple Pseudo-word Repeating

Lesson 4

Timed Activity (30 seconds)

The instructor makes sure everyone is comfortable and ready to begin work.

Instructor: *"I am going to say a made up word. Then, I want you to it to me exactly as I have said it to you. Let's try one for practice*

"woff" The class repeats the made-up word in unison. When everyone understands the requirements of the lesson, it is time for the timed lesson. If there is misunderstanding or confusion, keep practicing until you are sure everyone can follow the directions.

"Okay, we're ready to begin. Begin." The countdown timer is started.

1. brote
2. scall
3. crame
4. flipe
5. slup
6. frap
7. gribe
8. crainy
9. bive
10. longster
11. kreen
12. stornly
13. dellip
14. chanking
15. tumpy

Developing Expressive Language

Activity 4

Oral Expression

This activity is untimed. It is left up to instructor discretion how far to pursue a given conversation or line of thought. The purpose is to generate thinking and then to have students put their thoughts into words. It is important that everyone has the opportunity to express their thoughts. No one should be allowed to dominate the conversations.

1. Tell me a nonsense sound. Make up any sound that does not have meaning.

2. What do you do when you hear a word you do not know?

3. We have long words like rhinoceros and short words like it. We have long words like automobile and short words like my. Tell me a long word. Tell me a short word.

4. What do you think *(Instructor choose a pseudo-word)* could mean?

Building Vocabulary

Lesson 4

Snake

Instructor: *I am going to give you an animal name. Today's animal is a snake. I want you to think for a minute about snakes and then raise your hand to give me a word to tell me something you know about them. It can be their color, what they do, what they look like, where you can find them, their size and anything else about a snake that you can think of.*

Why don't some people like snakes?

Why are some people afraid of snakes?

How do they move?

Where do they live?

What do they eat?

What sizes are they?

Note: You can have the students draw a picture of any kind of snake doing something. Students then may stand at their desk or seat and show their picture and describe what they wrote

Developing Expressive Language

Games

Mother, May I?

One player plays the leader (mother, the father or the teacher.)

The others are the children. To begin the game, the leader stands at one end of the room or the playground and turns around facing away, while all the children line up at the other end.

The children take turns asking "Mother/Father, may I ____?" and asks the leader for permission to make a movement.

For example, one might ask, "Mother/Father/Teacher, may I take two steps forward?" The leader either replies, "Yes, you may" or "No, you may not do that, but you may _____ instead," and inserts his/her own suggestion.

The players usually move closer to the mother/father but are sometimes led farther away. Even if the leader makes a suggestion the player does not like, he or she must still perform it.

The first of the children to reach the location of the mother/father wins the game. That child then becomes the mother/father himself, the original mother/father becomes a child, and a new round begins.

Suggestions for the leader:

"Mother/Father/Teacher, may I ____?" blank include:

> Take (#) baby steps forward, giant steps forward, frog hops forward, kangaroo hops forward, etc.

Developing Expressive Language

Games

Simon Says

This game can be played anywhere, indoors or out. The leader is Simon and starts by saying to the group,

"Simon says, '<insert action here>.'"

Everyone must then do the action. However, if Simon makes an action request without saying, "Simon says" to begin the request, anyone who does that action is out. The last person still playing in the end will be Simon for the next round.

Developing Expressive Language

Singing

Hit the Road, Jack

This is another name song. It was written and performed in 1960 by Curtis Mayfield and later made famous by Ray Charles' rendition in 1961. It can be found by using your search engine. Practice before bringing the song and activity to the group.

These fun songs can be used year round, especially during transitions in your day, for fun.

"Oh Marci, Oh Marci – don't treat me so mean …"

"Oh Tyrone, Tyrone – don't treat me so mean …"

The child named can sing alone the part, "I just guess if you say so, I better pack my things and go …"

Then the group can shout, "That's right! Hit the road, Tyrone…"

Simple Sentence Repeating
Preparing for Lesson 5

Another early activity in phonological awareness involves simple sentence repeating. Simple sentence repeating is used to teach a child the concept of not only what a sentence is, but also the idea that words come together to make sentences. Thus, we teach the concept that there are a number of individual words within each sentence. This is used to assess and improve a child's familiarity with the sentence structure of spoken English. From there we go to further teach word identification and separation in the language.

The instructor of a small group for the upcoming sentence repeating activities needs to have the materials available to read, a countdown timer set to one minute and be prepared to move about the class observing and if necessary taking notes as the very short lesson proceeds. The children need to be carefully trained from the beginning in what responses are necessary and how the responses are to be given.

The tutor of a single child or very small group needs to sit across from the child or group. The countdown timer must be set to one-minute and the child or children calm and ready to proceed. The child should be very comfortable and relaxed. If per chance the timer and being timed is threatening a child, merely put the timer away or in a drawer where you can still see it and set the light to let you know when the minute is completed. For these exercises, the exact amount of time is not essential. A few seconds over the allotted time has little or no impact.

When a sentence is read, it must be read slowly with there being clear verbal distinctions between each word. The instructor of a group must be very careful to know that every student is prepared to take part in the activity as instructed. If one example does not suffice, do two or even three. The main focus needs to be on student achievement. When reading slowly, the instructor must continue to properly intonate. When the child or children respond, she must give immediate feedback, either praising the successful effort or correcting the student response. Immediate and focused correction is powerful.

*****

The instructor says, "*I am going to read you a sentence. I want you to repeat the sentence to me exactly as I have said it to you. Let's try one for practice.*" As the instructor reads intonation should be emphasized, even slightly exaggerated. The sentence should be read slowly. If you have a dialect or an accent, perhaps some time is needed to make sure you are correctly enunciating the sentence. Every effort has been made to avoid words that may prove tricky or difficult for our ELL students and teachers. However, this being a wonderful country of immense and growing diversity, there will be occasions of difficulty. Doing your utmost is what we desire, not perfection. These words are not an absolute script, it is most important that the student understand the directions. The timing of the actual activity should not begin until the instructor is assured everyone participating can follow the directions.

The instructor says, *"I love cheese pizza."* The individual or group should repeat the sentence exactly as it has been presented. The instructor of a group should be moving around the classroom and carefully listening to the student responses so as to ascertain those having any difficulties or not participating. Encouragement and coaching are encouraged.

The instructor will then say, *"Now, we'll begin. Remember, repeat the sentence exactly like I read it to you."*

The instructor sets the countdown timer and begins. If the exercise is completed correctly in less than one minute and there are no difficulties within the group, it is mastered. Each sentence not correctly repeated is an error. When a student or group master an exercise within the allotted time, a goal – leap – has been accomplished. Group work must be handled differently; the activity will be repeated daily until the instructor is certain that every student capable of mastering the lesson has indeed done so. When a goal has been made, the student(s) will begin on the next day to work on Lesson 2. Some lessons need only take one day, other lessons may require up to a week. Errors are immediately corrected and if felt necessary, remediated by a short lesson or practice after the timed exercise.

Simple Sentence Repeating

Lesson 5

Timed Activity (30 seconds)

The instructor makes sure everyone is comfortable and ready to begin work. The instructor should use exaggerated expression to model proper intonation, especially on the questions and exclamations.

Instructor: *I am going to say a sentence. Then, I want you to repeat the sentence to me exactly as I have said it to you. Let's try one for practice, "I love cheese pizza."*

The class repeats with the same intonation. When everyone understands the requirements of the lesson, it is time for the lesson. If there is misunderstanding or confusion you have another practice.

Instructor: *Now, we're ready to begin. Begin.*

1. I can hold my breath.
2. My ice cream is melting.
3. Let's go play in the rain.
4. The dragon sneezed.
5. The candy is gooey.
6. Why am I so hot today?
7. That tastes great!
8. Help, I am falling!
9. That potato salad made me sick.
10. I hate the smell of a wet dog.

Developing Expressive Language

Activity 5

Oral Expression

These questions and activities are designed to stimulate the child's brain while building language skills and depth of knowledge. Remember, you have a lot of options when choosing which questions to pursue with your student or class. If no interest is shown in a particular question, move on. These are untimed.

1. I can hold my breath. **Everyone hold your breath as I count to ten. Ten seconds seems like a long time when you're holding your breath, doesn't it?**

2. My ice cream is melting. **What do you think causes ice cream to melt? Why do you think Life Savers don't melt?**

3. Let's go play in the rain. **Why is it so much fun to play in the rain? Can you think of any dangers of playing in the rain?**

4. The dragon sneezed. **What can happen when a dragon sneezes?**

5. The candy is gooey. **What is it like when chocolate melts in your hand? What are some things you should not do when your hands are all chocolaty?**

6. Why am I so hot today? **What are some things you can you do to cool down on a hot summer day?**

7. That tastes great! **Some things taste good. But then, some things are better than good; they taste great. What do you think tastes great?**

8. Help, I'm falling! **Have you ever fallen off your bicycle? What happened?**

9. That potato salad made me sick. **What foods do you not like?**

10. I hate the smell of a wet dog. **Imagine for a minute the smell of a wet dog. Now, tell me about it.**

Building Vocabulary

Lesson 5

Dolphin

Instructor: *I am going to give you the name of an animal. Today's animal is the dolphin. I want you to think of this animal and then raise your hand to give me a word to tell me something you know about that animal. It can be the color, what the animal looks like, where you can find them, their size and anything else about that animal that you can think of. Let's do a practice one first.*

Where can you find dolphins?

What do they look like? What color are they?

What makes them special?

What do they eat?

What do they like to do?

Note: You can have the students draw a picture of a dolphin doing something. Students then may stand at their desk or seat and show their picture and describe what they wrote.

Developing Expressive Language

Singing

Have You Ever Seen
(Traditional Scottish Folk Song)

Have you ever seen a lassie, a lassie, a lassie …

Have you ever seen a lassie go this way and that?

Go this way and that way and this way and that way?

Have you ever seen a lassie go this way and that?

Have you ever seen a little boy, a l'il boy, a l'il boy …

Have you ever seen a little boy goes this way and that?

Go this way and that way and this way and that way?

Have you ever seen a little boy go this way and that?

Have you ever seen a l'il girl, a l'il girl, a little girl …

Have you ever seen a kitten, a kitten, a kitten …

Have you ever seen a puppy, a puppy, a puppy

Have you ever seen a calf ..

Have you ever seen a colt …

Have you ever seen a baby chick …

Have you ever seen a duckling …

Note: Have the children name other animals, or more specifically – baby animals.

Simple Sentence Repeating

Lesson 6

Timed Activity (one minute)

This exercise is to be done exactly as was done with Lesson 3.

Instructor: *Repeat the sentence to me exactly as I have said it to you. Let's try one for practice. "What is that silly monkey doing with that coconut?"*

Now, we'll begin. Repeat it the sentence exactly as you have heard it.

Begin.

1. The horse is running very fast.
2. A golden eagle screeched at the hunter.
3. The elephant was dancing.
4. I saw a ninja.
5. We had banana pudding instead of cake.
6. My friends jumped into the pool.
7. We are going to the beach for a week!
8. Why are so many clowns marching down the street?
9. That four-year old girl did a flip off the high dive.
10. The dragon blew fire at the lions.

Developing Expressive Language

Activity 6

1. The horse is running very fast. **Which animals can run faster than a horse? Can you run faster than a horse? Which is faster, a horse or a car?**

2. A golden eagle screeched at the hunter. **Name some really big birds. What are some other things that fly?**

3. The elephant was dancing. **What is the silliest dream you ever had? What is the silliest thing you have ever seen?**

4. I saw a ninja. **What is a ninja? How do they dress?**

5. We had banana pudding instead of cake. **What is your favorite dessert? Where is the best place to get it?**

6. My friends jumped into the pool. **What is so fun about jumping into a pool? Where is the closest swimming pool to your house?**

7. We are going to the beach for a week! **What are some of the things you like to do in summer?**

8. Why are so many clowns marching down the street? **Where are some of the places you can find clowns? Some people find clowns creepy, why? Draw a picture of a clown.**

9. That four-year old girl did a flip off the high dive. **Do you like swimming? Which animal do you think is the best swimmer in the world? Name some animals that you think cannot swim.**

10. The dragon blew fire at the lions. **What would happen if a dragon came to our playground or neighborhood? Would he or she be nice or bad? Why?**

Building Vocabulary

Lesson 6

Rabbit

Instructor: *I am going to give you some hints about an animal we all know. If you think you know which animal I am talking about, please don't say anything out loud, but raise your hand. I will then call on you and see what you think it is before I give another clue.*

Clue: I live in a hole. Who am I?

I have a cottontail. Who am I?

I hop.

I have long ears.

I eat carrots and other vegetables.

What else can you tell me about rabbits?

What makes a rabbit different from the other animals?

What are rabbits very good at?

What size are rabbits?

Are there any other animals that look like rabbits?

Are there any other animals that travel like rabbits?

Where do rabbits live?

Developing Expressive Language

Singing

My Bonnie
(Traditional British Folk Song)

My Bonnie lies over the ocean,

My Bonnie lies over the sea.

My Bonnie lies over the ocean

Oh, bring back my Bonnie to me.

Bring back, oh bring back

Bring back my Bonnie to me, to me.

Bring back, oh, bring back

Bring back my Bonnie to me.

Note: This song can include different members of the class, family, school and so forth. This affords the instructor another way to get creative, or to incorporate this song into the activities and lessons of the day. The song can be performed with physical activities.

Sentence Repeating

Preparing for Lesson 7

When we move from one sentence to two, we are working on more than memory. This gives us the opportunity to verbally show the split between sentences that will later demand punctuation so that our reading will make sense. So, as you read the sentences to the student, enunciate carefully. As the students respond, if you as instructor feel the sentences are not being repeated correctly or if there is difficulty from the children with the response, repeat with the timer running.

There will always be words some of the students do not understand. Remember, we are working with vocabulary development. The best way to deal with a definition is to nonchalantly define the word in the vernacular of the student. For example; with the question, "What ingredients do you like on your pizza." We let them know that the word ingredients means the different stuff you can put on a pizza like pepperoni, sausage, extra cheese, mushrooms, etc. They will get their new words via continued use. Keeping your vocabulary expectations high pays off.

Remember, we are not in a hurry. We are working for speed with accuracy; not speed for speed's sake.

Sentence Repeating

Lesson 7

Timed Activity (One Minute)

Instructor: *I am going to say two sentences. I want you to repeat them exactly as I have said them to you. Let's try one for practice. Try to repeat the words exactly as I told them to you.*

Practice: Look at that silly monkey. He is dressed up like a king.

Now, we'll begin. Remember to try to say it exactly like I say it to you. When the one-minute is over, we will talk about one of these.

1. It was very late at night. I heard a train whistle.
2. My tongue is very long. It can touch my nose.
3. Apple pie is my favorite! I love it with vanilla ice cream.
4. Cheese pizza is okay. I like it better with mushrooms.
5. I have a bicycle. I ride it every day.
6. I would like to have a pony. I would let you ride her.

Developing Expressive Language

Activity 7

1. It was very late at night. I heard a train whistle. **Imagine that you are in your bed getting ready to go to sleep. What are some of the sounds you may hear?**

2. My tongue is very long. It can touch my nose. **Stick out your tongue and try to touch your nose.** (If the student tries and fails, just stick out your tongue and touch your nose with your forefinger.)

3. Apple pie is my favorite! I love it with vanilla ice cream. **What dessert would you like for your birthday? How many friends would you like to have over for your birthday party?**

4. Cheese pizza is okay. I like it better with mushrooms. **What is your favorite kind of pizza?**

5. I have a bicycle. I ride it every a day. **As we grow and get bigger, we get to do more and more things. What is something that you are excited about doing soon?**

6. I would like to have a pony. I would let you ride her. **If you had your very own pony, where would she stay at night?**

Building Vocabulary

Lesson 7

Tiger

I am an animal that lives in the jungle. Who am I?

I am a member of the cat family. Who am I?

I am a big cat and can roar like a lion. Who am I?

I have stripes. Who am I?

Where can you go to find tigers?

What do they look like?

What do they eat?

What other animals look like tigers?

Are there any animals that you can think of that behave like tigers?

How big do you think a tiger is?

What kind of noise do tigers make?

Developing Expressive Language

Singing

For He's (She's) a Jolly Good Fellow
(Traditional English Folk Song)

For he's a jolly good fellow,
for he's a jolly good fellow,
for he's a jolly good fellow
    and nobody can deny.

And nobody can deny;
and nobody can deny;
For he's a jolly good fellow
    and nobody can deny!

The teacher can name someone in the class and sing, "For Jamie's a jolly good fellow, Jamie's a jolly good fellow … For she's a jolly good fellow, and nobody can deny."

Sentence Repeating

Lesson 8

Timed Activity (One Minute)

Instructor: *I am going to say two sentences. I want you to repeat them exactly as I have said them to you. Let's try one for practice.*

Practice: I am the captain of the soccer team. We are undefeated.

Now, we'll begin. Remember to repeat it exactly like I have said it to you.

1. A magician was at the party. She made a rabbit disappear.

2. My mother can do a back flip. Can yours?

3. I asked for a peanut butter ice cream cone. They only had vanilla.

4. Call 9-1-1 for help! There is smoke coming from that house!

5. The man was very tall. Sometimes he wishes that he was shorter.

6. I love chocolate covered cherries. I hate chocolate covered broccoli.

7. She was drinking her orange soda so fast it came bubbling out of her nose.

8. Is the moon really made out of green cheese? I don't believe it!

Developing Expressive Language

Activity 8

1. A magician was at the party. She made a rabbit disappear. **How do you think magic tricks work?**

2. My mother can do a back flip. Can yours? **Why can't most of our mothers do back flips?**

3. I asked for a peanut butter ice cream cone. They only had vanilla. **What is the best flavor of ice cream that you have *never* tasted?**

4. Call 9-1-1 for help! There is smoke coming from that house! **What are some good reasons to call for help?**

5. The man was very tall. Sometimes he wishes that he was shorter. **Why would a really tall man want to be shorter? Are you too tall, too short or just right?**

6. I love chocolate covered cherries. I hate chocolate covered broccoli. **If you had to chocolate cover something awful, what would you choose?**

7. She was drinking her orange soda so fast it came bubbling out of her nose. **Why do you think the soda came bubbling out her nose? Has that ever happened to you?**

8. Is the moon really made out of green cheese? I don't believe it! **If the moon were really made out of green cheese, what do you think it would taste like?**

Building Vocabulary

Lesson 8

Butterfly

I have wings but fly slowly. Who am I?

I am colorful. Who am I?

I am as light as a feather. Who am I?

I flutter from flower to flower? Who am I?

What is special about butterflies?

What other creatures are like butterflies?

What do you think they eat?

How big do they get?

Where do they go when it rains?

Why are they so pretty?

Developing Expressive Language

Singing

Skinny Marink
(Irish Folksong)

Skinny Marink a dink a dink,
Skinny Marink a doo,
I love you.

Skinny Marink a dink a dink,
Skinny Marink a doo,
I love you.

I love you in the morning
and in the afternoon.
I love in the evening
 and underneath the moon.

Oh, Skinny Marink a dink a dink,
Skinny Marink a doo,
I love you.

Tapping Words

Preparing for Lesson 9

Our objective in this lesson is to teach through action that sentences are made up of words. This is not intuitive for a young child. By teaching this and making it fun, we are paving the way for more efficient reading. We teach children to realize that words are made up of several sounds and syllables by showing them how to recognize words by clapping or tapping them. Tapping can be performed by clapping hands or with an object such as a pencil or chopstick. Tapping should be gentle and with a group in unison. Activities with action allow our students to become more engaged and thus more acquainted with what exactly a word is.

When we model the tapping of the words in a sentence, work very deliberately so that the children can see the correspondence between the tap and the word. For "I hit the ball," I leave about a half second pause between each word as I tap. When they are responding, I want the group to tap in unison with my reading of the sentence.

When you hear an error, repeat until you think the group has the idea and then move on. The activity only takes one minute.

Tapping Words

Lesson 9 (One Minute)

Timed Activity

Instructor: *I am going to say a sentence. I want you to repeat the sentence and use your index finger to make a tap for each word as you say it.*

The instructor says the sentence, *"Let me show you how to do it."* Each word must be clearly enunciated while a nice loud tap is made. Remember, this is our first lesson in distinguishing words. Your tapping has to get that idea across. When you model or correct the tapping, make sure to emphasize a tap coordinated with each word.

Whenever you hear a mistake, make sure to <u>immediately correct and model the correct response</u>. With the group, this will involve carefully issuing the prompt and even clarifying the expectations. The timer keeps on going. Tap as you say each word. For instance, if a student gave three taps for the word hamburger, you would say, "Hamburger is one word, one thing," and show it as one tap.

Now try one: *(Remember to say the sentence slowly and clearly while tapping.)*

My hair is curly. (4 taps) Be careful for those who tap twice for curly, we are tapping words not syllables.

Let's begin.

1. Hop like a kangaroo. (4 taps)
2. Look at that big, hairy spider! (6 taps)
3. Sissy can climb a tree. (5 taps)
4. I can swim. (3 taps)
5. I want to play in snow. (6 taps)
6. I want to swim with a dolphin. (7 taps)
7. Do sharks like candy? (4 taps)
8. I have a pet turtle. (5 taps)

Developing Expressive Language
Activity 9

1. Hop like a kangaroo.

   Why do you think kangaroos can hop better than turtles? Can you think of anything that turtles do better than kangaroos?

2. Look at that big, hairy spider!

   What insects live in your yard? Are you afraid of any of them? What are the names of some insects that you like?

3. Sissy can climb a tree.

   What can you climb?

4. I can swim.

   Hold your breath as I count to twenty. When completed, the instructor asks, "What were you thinking as I counted? "

5. I want to play in snow.

   Which is more fun, playing in the snow or swimming in a pool? Why?

6. I want to swim with a dolphin.

   Describe a dolphin. Draw a picture of a dolphin.

7. Do sharks like candy?

   Who should worry about sharks? Who needs to worry about sharks?

8. I have a pet turtle.

   What are some things that would make a turtle get scared and hide in its shell?

Building Vocabulary

Lesson 9

Kangaroo

I really can hop. Who am I?

I live in Australia. Who am I?

I walk or hop on two legs. Who am I?

I have a pouch where I carry my baby. Who am I?

Where do kangaroos live?

Is there anything special about kangaroos?

What color are they?

What do you think they eat?

Do kangaroos get along with people?

Developing Expressive Language

Singing

The Itsy Bitsy Spider
(American Folk Song)

The Itsy Bitsy Spider
climbed up the water spout.
Down came the rain,
and washed the spider out.
Out came the sun,
and dried up all the rain.
And the itsy bitsy spider
climbed up the spout again.

Students should be encouraged to do the activities of the little spider as they sing.

Sentence Repeating

Lesson 10

Timed Activity (One Minute)

Instructor: *I am going to say a sentence. I want you to repeat the sentence and use your index finger to make a tap for each word as you say it.*

Practice: My father is six feet tall. (6 taps)

I am going to say a sentence. I want you to repeat the sentence and use your index finger to make a tap for each word as you say it.

1. I do not like winter. (5 taps)
2. We are having asparagus for dinner. (6 taps)
3. I really want to do it! (6 taps)
4. Spin it round and round. (5 taps)
5. Your nose is running. (4 taps)
6. What is that in your refrigerator? (6 taps)
7. Is that really your nose? (5 taps)
8. My baby brother is a pest. (6 taps)
9. Cross your fingers. (3 taps)
10. I am not afraid of ghosts. (6 taps)

Developing Expressive Language

Activity 10

1. I do not like winter. **If someone does not like winter, which season or time of the year do you suppose they would like? What is your favorite time or season of the year? Why?**

2. We are having asparagus for dinner. **What is asparagus? How does it taste? Our food comes in a lot of colors. Name some food that is green ... red .... yellow .... white ...**

3. I really want to do it! **Name something that you have done that you never want to do again.**

4. Spin it round and round. **Why do you think people get dizzy when they go round and round? Describe how you feel when you're dizzy.**

5. Your nose is running. **Before you get a cold, often your nose runs. What other symptoms come with a cold?**

6. What is that in your refrigerator? **What are some things you have in your refrigerator at home? Why are refrigerators cold?**

7. Is that really your nose? **Why do clowns have red bulbs for their noses? What all does a nose do?**

8. My baby brother is a nuisance. **Why don't big kids like being called babies? What are some of the differences between babies and big kids?**

9. Cross your fingers. **Show me how to cross your fingers. Why do people do that? Everyone, cross your eyes!**

10. I am not afraid of ghosts. **What are some things that make you afraid?**

Building Vocabulary

Lesson 10

Shark

I live in the ocean and my skin is like gray leather. Who am I?

People are very afraid of me. Who am I?

I swim very fast and can eat and digest just about anything. Who am I?

My fin showing in the water, warns people that I am near. Who am I?

Why are people afraid of sharks?

Where do sharks live?

What do you think they eat?

What color are they?

How big are they?

Why do they have so many teeth?

Developing Expressive Language

Singing

My Hand on My Head
German American Folk Song

My hand on my head, what have I here?

This is my head-thinker, my Mama dear

Head-thinker, head-thinker, Nicky nicky noo

That's what they taught me in school.   Hi Ya!

My hand on my eyes, what have I here?

These are my eye-lookers, my Mama dear.

Eye-lookers, head-thinker,   Nicky nicky noo

That's what they taught me in school. Hi Ya!

My hand on my nose, what have I here?

This is my nose-smeller, my Mama dear

Nose-smeller, eye-lookers, head-thinker, Nicky nicky noo

That's what they taught me in school.   Hi Ya!

My hand on my mouth,, what have I here?

This is my mouth-taster, My Mama dear

Mouth-taster, nose-smeller, eye-lookers, head-thinker, Nicky nicky noo

That's what they taught me in school.   Hi Ya!

Put my hand on my hand, What have I here?

This is my hand-toucher, my Mama dear

Hand-toucher, mouth-taster, nose-smeller, eye-lookers, head-thinker, Nicky nicky noo

That's what they taught me in school. Hi ya!

Tapping Words

Lesson 11

Timed Lesson (One Minute)

Instructor: *I am going to say a sentence. I want you to repeat the sentence and use your index finger to make a tap for each word as you say it.*

Practice: My father is six feet tall. (6 taps)

I am going to say a sentence. I want you to repeat the sentence and use your index finger to make a tap for each word.

Reminder: If there is a mistake, <u>you immediately correct it with modeling</u>: how it should be done or sound. Tap as you say each word. For instance, if there are three taps given for tricycle. You would say, "Tricycle is one word, one thing," and show it as one tap. Compound words such as basketball and tonight can cause particular difficulties.

Instructor: N*ow, we'll begin. Remember to try to say it exactly like I say it to you while you tap each word.*

1. The chimps were riding tricycles. (5 taps)
2. Keep the pickles off my hamburger! (6 taps)
3. We built a hut in the forest. (7 taps)
4. "Good try!" shouted the coach. (5 taps)
5. Why do my feet smell so bad? (7 taps)
6. Let's go to the basketball game tonight. (7 taps)
7. Are there horses in the ocean? (6 taps)
8. My French uncle actually eats snails. (6 taps)
9. We were up so high my ears popped. (8 taps)
10. That pirate doesn't have teeth. (5 taps)

Developing Expressive Language

Activity 11

1. The baboons were riding tricycles. **What could be sillier than a baboon riding a tricycle?**

2. Keep the pickles off my hamburger! **What do you like on your hamburger? What are some things you do not like on your burger?**

3. We built a hut in the forest. **What is your favorite piece of playground equipment? Why do boys and girls like to climb trees?**

4. "Good try!" shouted the coach. **What is a coach? Why do coaches often shout so loudly?**

5. Why do my feet smell so bad? **What is it about some people's feet that can make them stink so bad? What is the best smell in the world?**

6. Let's go to the basketball game tonight. **What would you like to do tonight? What are some things you love to do outside?**

7. Are there horses in the ocean? **Besides fish, what lives in water?**

8. My French uncle actually eats snails. **People eat snails and frogs. Why? Would you?**

9. We were up so high my ears popped. **If you looked out the window of an airplane, what do you think you would see?**

10. That pirate doesn't have teeth. **Tell me what a pirate looks like. How could you tell a woman pirate from a man pirate? What are some things that pirates do? Draw a mean pirate.**

Building Vocabulary

Lesson 11

Monkey

I live in the trees of the jungle but am not a bird. Who am I?

I have very long arms and a tail. Who am I?

I like to eat coconuts and bananas. Who am I?

I have great balance and can swing from tree to tree. Who am I?

Why do people laugh at monkeys?

Where do monkeys live?

What do monkeys like to do?

What do you think monkeys eat?

What other animals do monkeys resemble?

Developing Expressive Language

Singing

Brother John
(French Folk Round)

Are you sleeping, are you sleeping

Brother John, Brother John?

Morning bells are ringing, morning bells are ringing

Ding dong ding; Ding dong ding!

Frère Jacques, Frère Jacques,

Dormez vous? Dormez vous?

Sonnez les matines , Sonnez les matines,

Din, din, don! Din, din, don!

This can also be changed into a name song. The instructor will have to make sure they can fit the name of the child into the rhythm of the song. Don't forget to teach this as a round. The instructor will have to be musically and rhythmically creative to have some names fit smoothly within the tune of the song.

Making Words from Syllables

Preparing for Lesson 12

Syllabication, breaking words into syllables, is a pre-reading skill with major ramifications in reading and spelling. Syllable awareness and basic phonics skills give a child powerful reading skills when encountering new words. This is the initial step in that process.

We tell the students that our longer words are made up of syllables. We can tap these syllables just like we tapped the word before. When introducing a new concept you do your best to give instructions so that the student has an excellent chance of mastering the skill early.

Making Words from Syllables
Lesson 12

Timed Activity (30 seconds)

Instructor: *I am going to split a word into its parts. I want you to put those parts together and tell me the word. When we finish, we'll talk a bit about a couple of the words. Let's practice:*

Practice:

(croc … o …. dile)   crocodile

(prin …. cess)   princess

Ready? (The instructor must say each syllable with a very distinct pause between each, making certain the students say the word as a single entity, not splitting it.)

1. pan … cake   pancake
2. straw … ber … ry   strawberry
3. pump … kin   pumpkin
4. un … i … corn   unicorn
5. rock … et   rocket
6. fire … crack … er   firecracker
7. ma … chine   machine
8. cook … ies   cookies
9. out … side   outside
10. dis … gust … ing   disgusting

Developing Expressive Language
Activity 12

1. pancake – **Name three toppings that we put on a pancake. When is the best time to eat a pancake?**

2. strawberry – **How is a strawberry like an apple? How are strawberries and apples different?**

3. pumpkin – **Why do people carve pumpkins at Halloween to look so mean? Draw a picture of a Halloween pumpkin. Why do you think we call them jack-o-lanterns?**

4. unicorn - **If you were going to go out and find a unicorn, where would you begin your search? Name some other animals that have horns. Why do you think they have horns? What would you look like with some nice big horns? Draw that picture.**

5. rocket – **What does a rocket do? Draw a picture of a rocket taking off. Don't forget the flames.**

6. firecracker – **How can firecrackers be dangerous? How do you feel when lots of fireworks are going off? What sounds do they make?**

7. machine – **What is a machine? What is the biggest machine you can think of? Are there some machines in your house?**

8. cookies – **What kind of cookies would you put in your cookie jar? Where is the best place to get cookies?**

9. outside - **What do you like to do when you go outside? Which is more fun, playing outside with your friends or watching television all by yourself? Why?**

10. disgusting – **Disgusting means really nasty. What are some disgusting foods you can think of?**

Building Vocabulary

Lesson 12

Cow

I am a large farm animal. Who am I?

I eat grass. Who am I?

I am never in a hurry. Who am I?

When I am milked, I may moo. Who am I?

Why do you think cows moo?

Where can you find a herd of cows?

What do cows do most of the day?

What do cowboys ride? Why don't cowboys ride cows?

What other animals resemble a cow?

Developing Expressive Language

Singing

One, Two
(American Folk Song)

One, two, buckle my shoe;
Three, four, shut the door;
Five, six, pick up sticks;
Seven, eight, lay them straight;
Nine, ten, a big fat hen!
Now it's time to sing again!

Have the child or children pretend to do the actions as you recite or sing the poem.

Breaking Words into Syllables

Lesson 13

Timed Activity (One Minute)

Instructor: *I am now going to say a word. I want you to break each word into its parts out loud while you make a tap for each part you hear in the word. These parts are called syllables.*

Lets practice some:

television	(tel … e …. vi …s ion)	(4 taps)
radio	(ra …. di …. o)	(3 taps)

Ready? Begin.

1.	motor	mo … tor	2 taps
2.	banana	ba … na… na	3 taps
3.	breakfast	break …. fast	2 taps
4.	pencil	pen … cil	2 taps
5.	stadium	sta…di … um	3 taps
6.	telephone	tel … e … phone	3 taps
7.	London	Lon - don	2 taps
8.	carpet	car … pet	2 taps
9.	weather	wea … ther	2 taps
10.	stump	stump	1 tap

Developing Expressive Language
Activity 13

1. motor: **Name some things that have motors. Name some moving things that do not have motors.**

2. banana: **How is a banana different from an apple? How is it the same? What can we do with bananas?**

3. breakfast: **What did you have for breakfast this morning? What do you think we having for lunch tomorrow?**

4. pencil: **How are pencils different from pens? How are they different from crayons?**

5. stadium: **Many sports are sports are played in stadiums. What sport would your family like to go watch at a stadium?**

6. telephone: **If you could call someone up on the telephone right now, who would it be? What would you say?**

7. London: **London is the name of a city in England. You may have sang the song "London Bridge is Falling Down." Have you ever been to a really big city? Which one? What did you do or see? How did you get there?**

8. carpet: **What is another word for carpet? Why do you think people put carpets on their floor? Why aren't there carpets on the ceiling?**

9. weather: **Tell me about the weather outside right now.**

10. stump: **When a big tree is cut down a stump is left. What are some things you can do on a stump?**

Building Vocabulary

Lesson 13

Milk

I want you to think of milk and then raise your hand to tell me something you know about milk. It can be the color, where you can find it, what it tastes like, what you can do with it, what kind of milk do you get from brown or black cows, or anything else about milk that you can think of.

What are some things that have milk in them?

What are some things made from milk?

When is the best time to drink milk?

What kinds of milk are there?

If white cows give us white milk, what kind of milk do we get from brown cows?

Developing Expressive Language

Singing

Hokey Pokey
(© Sony/ATV Music)

This is a fun dance activity for the entire class. When children combine singing with dance, the entire brain is engaged. These activities are enormously beneficial for the language growth of young students.

Find the song and dance on your search engine and master it before teaching the class.

Section II

Building Words, Sentences and Vocabulary

Section II

Building Words, Sentences and Vocabulary

From understanding what a word is, we begin moving the students into working with words in sentences. The more words we have in our receptive vocabulary, the better and more complex the sentences we can construct. With the young student, building and using an extensive vocabulary consistently will greatly enhance their ability, especially in reading comprehension, over the next few years.

During the timed activity of a small group, it remains important for the instructor to move about the class so that she can hear every student's responses and be able to mentally or physically note the level of participation from each student. If she hears a student is having difficulty, immediate correction while standing near the student is required. Tone of voice (never threatening or aggressive) is important during correction. Voice can be punishing in many ways. Punishment, no matter how subtle, impedes motivation and performance. The tone of voice needs to be encouraging or just matter of fact. If the difficulties seem considerable, after activity tutoring is recommended. This could also be done at home if the parent has purchased a copy of the material or the instructor has provided a practice lesson or activity for the student.

The lessons in this section should be relatively easy for the students to master in less than a week per lesson. Any song from the repertoire that is being built can be used. Simon Says and May I can be used with creative variations to continue work in following directions.

Forming Words, then Sentences

Preparing for Lesson 14

With this lesson we are going to reverse from a word being broken into syllables to make a word from the parts. Then, we are going to have them practice putting that word into a meaningful sentence.

The instructor of a group will have some options on this activity. It is okay if the entire group says their sentence at the same time. This may confuse an instructor but it will not be confusing to most of the children. If this does not fit into your style of teaching, then it is okay for you to point to a student to compose the sentence in their mind and present it. It must be a sentence of meaning. The instructor can enhance the student response as a comment.

Example: Student: *The pirate is on a ship.*

Teacher: *Yes! The pirate is on his ship sailing to Bermuda to bury his treasure.*

Forming Words, then Sentences

Lesson 14

Timed Activity (One Minute)

Instructor: *I am going to break a word into its parts ... these parts are called syllables. I want you to put them together into the word and then use it in a short sentence showing that you know what the word means.*

Example: pi ... rate   (pirate)   The pirate has a peg leg.

           bull ... frog   (bullfrog)   The bullfrog croaked.

Now, try one for practice.

           surf ... ing   (surfing)   ....

Ready?

1. Sat ... ur ... day
2. bi ... cy .... cle
3. com ... put ... er
4. for .... est
5. Sep ... tem ... ber
6. el – e – men – ta – ry

This lesson may take a few times for a class or student to master. The organizational skills gained are considerable.

Developing Expressive Language

Language Activity 14

1. Saturday – **What are some things you like to do on Saturday mornings? What day comes after Saturday?**

2. bicycle – **What can you do on your bicycle? Why do some bicycles have training wheels?**

3. computer – **What are some of the things you can you do on a computer? Where can you find computers?**

4. forest – **What are some animals that live in the forest? What animals live near you?**

5. September – **September is the first month of autumn or fall. One thing that happens are that the weather becomes cooler. What are some of the other things that happen during fall?**

6. elementary – **What is an elementary school?**

Building Vocabulary

Lesson 14

Peanut Butter

Instructor: *Today we will talk about peanut butter. I want you to think quietly about peanut butter and then raise your hand to give me a word to tell me something you know about it. It can be the color, what it looks like, where you can find it, what do we do with it, and so forth.*

What are some of the ways you eat peanut butter?

What is good with peanut butter?

How do you think they make peanut butter?

Besides bread, what can you put it on?

My sister believes in peanut butterflies. What could those possibly be?

Developing Expressive Language

Singing

The Mulberry Bush
(English Folk Song)

Here we go round the mulberry bush, the mulberry bush, the mulberry bush.
Here we go round the mulberry bush, on a cold and frosty morning.

This is the way we wash our clothes, wash our clothes, wash our clothes.
This is the way we wash our clothes on a cold and frosty morning.

This is the way we wash our hair, wash our hair, wash our hair.
This is the way we wash our hair on a cold and frosty morning.

This is the way we hammer the nail, hammer the nail, hammer the nail.
This is the way we hammer the nail on a cold and frosty morning.

This is the way we stir the pot, stir the pot, stir the pot.
This is the way we stir the pot on a cold and frosty morning.

This is the way we jump real high, jump real high, jump real high.
This is the way we jump real high on a cold and frosty morning.

Here we go round the mulberry bush, the mulberry bush, the mulberry bush.
Here we go round the mulberry bush, on a cold and frosty morning

Note: Students should be encouraged to mimic the activity as they sing.

Defining Words

Preparing for Lesson 15

Words have meaning. To use words we must know what they mean. To understand sentences we must have the knowledge of working with words conversationally. To own a word, you must have experience in using that word. The thought that it takes to define and then use a word is neurologically beneficial for a young student.

This lesson may very well take up to a week for a student or class to be able to master. This is a powerful exercise in developing early thinking skills. This may prove very challenging for some students. You must be patient if you encounter difficulties. Think of it this way: if the student appears to be having difficulty with this lesson, understand that you are now working in an area that will prove crucial to the child's early reading development.

As we move along with these exercises, you may eventually hit a place where the student is not developmentally ready for the lesson. There is no inherent frustration with children when they encounter difficult language. I believe these anxieties are often socially induced. So, it is very critical for your attitude to always be positive and for you to always be patient. When you hit the task that is impossible for the student, acknowledge it and set your goals. It is our goal with these exercises to stimulate a student's mind in language as much as we can. The task will not be frustrating if you coach and tell them the thinking process orally as you give practice demonstrations.

In the following lesson you are going to be giving the student a word or two and have it defined for you. Then the student or students are to use the word in a sentence. Unless the answer is completely off course, it is not a mistake. Let the child or children think and work out the words. Give a group ten seconds or so to think and then raise their hands if they would like to respond.

If help is needed, it should be done carefully to elicit the response from the student rather than giving them the answer. This lesson is primarily intended to have children think about words and what they mean; to use their minds to respond. If the answer is too short or inadequate, help them elaborate. Do not always choose the first hands up. Allow children to elaborate upon their first response.

Defining Words
Lesson 15

Timed Activity (One Minute)

Instructor: *I am going to tell you a word or two. I want you to in your own words define or describe what I am talking about or tell me what you think it is. I am not asking for a lot of words in your answer.*

Here's an example.

jet – You could tell me it is a fast airplane.

tiger – You could tell me that it is a large cat with stripes.

Now, you try one for practice: bicycle ...

Okay. Are you ready?

Let's go.

1. car
2. sandwich
3. telephone
4. television
5. grass
6. whale
7. shirt
8. carpet
9. mother
10. lake

Developing Expressive Language

Language Activity 15

1. car: If you could choose to have a really neat car, what kind would you choose? What kind of car do you think your grandmother would choose?

2. sandwich: Where is the best place to get a sandwich?

3. telephone: If I asked you to call someone on the phone right now, who would you call and what would you talk about?

4. television: What is your favorite television program? Who else in your family likes it? Tell me a television show you do not like.

5. grass: Name some animals that eat grass. If you saw a person eating grass, what would you do?

6. whale: What do you think killer whales eat? Whales live in the ocean. What other large animals live in the ocean.

7. shirt: Describe your favorite shirt.

8. carpet: If you spilled milk on your carpet, how would you clean it?

9. mother: What is your mother's favorite thing to do? What color is her hair?

10. lake: What are some fun things to do in the water in summer? Can you do anything with water in the winter?

Building Vocabulary

Lesson 15

Potato

Instructor: *Today, we are going to talk about the potato. I want you to think quietly about potatoes and then raise your hand to give me a word or two to tell me something you know about them. It can be the color, what they look like, where you can find them, what you can do with them and so forth.*

How many different ways can you think of cooking potatoes?

Where can you go to get some potatoes?

Where can you go to get cooked potatoes?

Where do potatoes grow? What other foods grow under the ground?

What size are potatoes?

Developing Expressive Language

Game

Potatoes

One Potato, Two Potato

Three Potato, Four

Five Potato, Six Potato

Seven Potato, More

Have the students sit in a circle. Everyone should hold out one fist (or two) into the circle. A leader then goes around the circle and touches the top of each person's fist with his or her fist as the students recite the "One Potato, Two Potatoes" rhyme. When the rhyme reaches, "More!" the child whose fist the leader bumps is "out" and takes their hand out of the circle. Start the rhyme again from the next person.

Look up "one potato, two potato" in your search engine.

Developing Expressive Language

Singing

Shoo Fly
1869 – T. Brigham Bishop

Shoo fly, don't bother me.

Shoo fly, don't bother me.

Shoo fly, don't bother me.

'Cause I belong to somebody.

I feel, I feel, I feel,

I feel like a morning star.

I feel, I feel, I feel,

I feel like a morning star.

Oh! Shoo fly, don't bother me.

Shoo fly, don't bother me.

Shoo fly, don't bother me.

'Cause I belong to somebody!

Vocabulary Building

Lesson 16

Timed Activity (One Minute)

Instructor: *I am going to tell you a word or two. I want you to, in your own words, describe what I am talking about or tell me what you think it is. I am not asking for a sentence but a description. These will be action words about things you can do. I just want you to tell me about the action.*

Here's an example.

smile– a face I make when I'm happy

throw – to take a ball or something and toss it somewhere

Now, you try one for practice: cry

Okay. Are you ready?

Let's go.

1. jump
2. sing
3. grab
4. fall
5. eat
6. drive
7. build
8. cough
9. work
10. laugh

Note for the instructor: Unless the answer is completely off course, it is not to be considered a mistake. Let the child think and work out the words and their meanings. If help is needed, it should be done carefully to help elicit the response from the child rather than your giving them the answer. Sometimes you must be patient and allow the answer to be worked out. This lesson is to have children think about words and what they mean. If the answer is too short or inadequate, help them elaborate.

Developing Expressive Language

Language Activity 16

1. jump – How high can you jump?
2. sing – Choose any song you can think of and sing me a little piece of it.
3. grab - Everyone, make a fist. Tell me how you did it.
4. fall – What happens when you fall down?
5. eat – How many times a day do you eat? Name something you should not eat.
6. drive – Of all the things in the world, what do you think would be most fun to drive and why?
7. build – What would I need if I wanted to build a really neat tree house?
8. cough– Too much smoke can make me cough.
9. throw – What are some things you can throw?
10. laugh – What could I do to make you laugh out loud?

Vocabulary Building

Lesson 16

Apples

Instructor: *Today we will talk about apples. I want you to think quietly about apples and then raise your hand and tell me something you know about them. It can be the color or the colors, what they look like, where you can find them, what are some of the things we do we do with them, and so forth.*

Where do we find apples?

What colors do apples come in?

What are some very sweet things made with apples?

Besides eating apples, what else can we do with them?

What other fruits have similarities to apples? *(Example: peaches are round. Cherries are red.)*

Developing Expressive Language
Singing
Joy to the World

Jeremiah was a bullfrog, was a good friend of mine

I never understood a single word he said

Cause he wasn't smart like ole Einstein

    He wasn't smart like ole Einstein

        Singing joy to the world, all the boys and girls

        Joy to the fishes in the deep blue sea, joy to you and me

If I were the king of the world, tell you what I'd do

I'd put all the cars in a parking lot, and I'd play in the street with you

    Yes, I'd play in the street with you

        Singing joy to the world, all the boys and girls

        Joy to the fishes in the deep blue sea, joy to you and me

You know I love our playground, I love to have my fun

I'm a high kite flyer and a skateboard rider. I love to play in the sun!

    Yes, I'd play in the street with you

        Singing joy to the world, all the boys and girls

        Joy to the fishes in the deep blue sea, joy to you and me

© *Taken from the song by Hoyt Axton (1970)*

Modifications by Kenneth U. Campbell (2013)

Vocabulary Building

Lesson 17

Timed Activity (One Minute)

Instructor: *I am going to tell you a word or two. I want you to in your own words describe what I am talking about or tell me what you think it is. I am not asking for a sentence but a description. These words will be things you should know about. Tell me what the word means.*

Here are some examples:

Eye - the part of my body for sight or what I see with

ice cream – a cold dessert of frozen milk and sugar

Now, you try one for practice: tree

Okay. Are you ready?

Let's begin.

1. grocery store (a place where we buy food)
2. fairy tale (a bed time story)
3. zoo (a place with many animals)
4. mouse (a small, furry animal)
5. birthday party (friends come by with presents and have cake)
6. sky (the blue above us)
7. bathtub (where I wash up at night)
8. crash (a banging where things break)
9. hurricane (a bad storm with wind and rain)
10. hurt (make something feel bad)

Developing Expressive Language
Language Activity 17

1. grocery store – **What is something you cannot buy in a grocery store?**

2. fairy tale – **What is your favorite bed time story and why do you like that one?**

3. zoo – **If we could go to the zoo right now, what animal would you go see first? Why?**

4. mouse – **What would your mom do if she saw a mouse in your house? What would your grandfather do?**

5. birthday party – **Where do you want to have your next birthday party? Why there? What kind of cake would you want?**

6. sky – **What are some things you can look up to the sky and see?**

7. bathtub – **If you could take a bath in something besides water, what would it be?**

8. crash – **What are some things that can crash?**

9. hurricane – **What is the scariest thing about a hurricane? Where do they happen?**

10. hurt – **What are some things that really hurt?**

Building Vocabulary

Lesson 17

Cereal

Instructor: *Today, we are going to talk about cereal. As you know, there are a lot of different kinds of cereal. I want you to think quietly about cereal and then raise your hand to give me a word or sentence to tell me something that you know about cereal. It can be the colors, the ingredients, the different flavors, the different names they give cereals and so forth.*

Where do you buy cereal?

What do you think they make cereal from?

Why do you think many kinds of cereals have so many colors?

When is cereal usually eaten?

What other foods do you eat with cereal?

What are some things you can put in your cereal to make it taste better?

Developing Expressive Language

Singing

The Bear Went Over the Mountain
German-American Folk Song

The bear went over the mountain.

The bear went over the mountain.

The bear went over the mountain to see what he could see.

And all that he could see;

and all that he could see;

was the other side of the mountain,

the other side of the mountain,

the other side of the mountain was all that he could see!

This is the tune of *"For He's a Jolly Good Fellow"*

Note: Children may mimic the actions of the bear as they sing. Verses can be added about other things the bear can cross as in "the bear went across the river, the bear went across the river…" or you can sing about something the bear could do as in, "The bear went through our garbage, the bear went through our garbage, to see what he could find. And all that he could find… was a bunch of our garbage, was a bunch of garbage…"

Vocabulary Building

Lesson 18

Timed Activity (One Minute)

Instructor: *I am going to tell you a word or two. I want you to in your own words describe what I am talking about or tell me what you think it is. I am not asking for a sentence but a description or your telling me what it means.*

Here are some examples:

sleep over– friends come over to have fun and spend the night

bicycle rack – the place at school where you lock up and park your bike

Now, you try one for practice: ice cream cone

Okay. Are you ready? Let's begin.

1. candy store
2. washing machine
3. bedroom
4. door
5. tool box
6. the weekend
7. woodpecker
8. far away
9. great day
10. make-believe

Developing Expressive Language

Language Activity 18

1. candy store – **If you owned a candy store, what would you sell in it?**

2. washing machine – **How would we get our clothes clean if we did not have washing machines?**

3. bedroom– **What are some things in a bedroom?**

4. door – **Close your eyes and imagine your front door for a minute. Think about the color and anything else that might be on it. Now describe it for me. Draw your front door. Color it. Draw it again and make it a color you would like.**

5. tool box – **Almost every house or garage has a toolbox. Name something that must be in it. Name something that would be unusual to find in a toolbox.**

6. the weekend – **What is your favorite thing about the weekend?**

7. woodpecker – **Woodpeckers use their tough beaks to peck at trees. Why do you think they are they doing this?**

8. far away – **If you had to go somewhere far, far away, where would you choose? Why? Who would you want to go with you?**

9. great day – **What could make this day, today, great?**

10. make-believe – **Who would you most want to meet in the world of make-believe? Who would you most definitely not want to meet in that world of make-believe? Why?**

Vocabulary Building

Lesson 18

Broccoli

Instructor: *Today, I am going to talk with you about everyone's favorite vegetable, broccoli. I want you to think for a minute or so about broccoli and then raise your hand to give me a word or sentence to tell me something about it. It can be the color, what it tastes like, where you can find it, what do we do with it, and so forth.*

When people say that broccoli is good for you, what do they mean?

Where do we go to buy broccoli?

Is there anywhere you can get broccoli already cooked, precooked?

Name some other green vegetables.

Is there a vegetable that to you tastes a bit like broccoli. Which ones?

Developing Expressive Language

Singing

Dem Bones
African American Folk Spiritual

Chorus: Dem bones, dem bones, dem dry bones,

Dem bones, dem bones, dem dry bones,

Dem bones, dem bones, dem dry bones,

Now shake dem skeleton bones!

    The toe bone's connected to the foot bone,

    The foot bone's connected to the ankle bone,

    The ankle bone's connected to the leg bone,

    Now shake dem skeleton bones!

    The leg bone's connected to the knee bone,

    The knee bone's connected to the thigh bone,

    The thigh bone's connected to the hip bone,

    Now shake dem skeleton bones!

Chorus:

    The hip bone's connected to the back bone

    The back bone's connected to the neck bone,

    The neck bone's connected to the head bone,

    Now shake dem skeleton bones!

    The finger bone's connected to the hand bone,

    The hand bone's connected to the arm bone,

    The arm bone's connected to the shoulder bone,

    Now shake dem skeleton bones!

Chorus:

Turning Phrases into Sentences

Lesson 19

Timed Activity (One Minute)

Instructor: *I am going to give you two words. I want you to use them in a good sentence or good sentences that make sense. You must keep the two words together.*

Examples: wet dog   *I do not like the smell of a **wet dog**.*

             French poodle   The **French poodle** costs too much money.

1. truck driver
2. seven girls
3. green teeth
4. hungry bear
5. purple cow
6. green goo
7. funny looking
8. lazy kitten

Note: If you get to the bottom of the page and there is still time remaining, go back up to number 1 and continue.

Expressive Language

Language Activity 19

Instructor: *Answer these questions as best you can.*

1. What are some things you need to know if you are going to be a truck driver?

2. If there were seven girls playing outside, what do you think they would be playing?

3. If you do not brush your teeth, do you believe they will turn green? Why do we brush our teeth?

4. If a bear were really hungry, what do you think he would want?

5. How could a cow be purple?

6. There is a TV show where they pour green goo on people. Everyone laughs. Why?

7. What do clowns do to make themselves so funny looking?

8. What is the laziest animal on earth? Why do you say that?

Vocabulary Building

Lesson 19

Carrots

Instructor: *What is orange and long and grows under the ground? Yes, a carrot! I want you to think quietly about carrots and then raise your hand to give me a word to tell me something you know about them.*

How have you eaten carrots?

Where do you get carrots?

What sound does a carrot make when you bite into it?

How do carrots grow?

Draw a picture of a carrot. It is orange. Don't forget the green top.

Developing Expressive Language

Singing

The Little Green Frog
(American Folk Song – Origins Unknown)

Gink Gank went the little green frog one day
Gink Gank went the little green frog
Gink Gank went the little green frog one day
And his eyes went gink-gank-gunk

But we know frogs go
Lod de dah de dah
Lod de dah de dah
Lod de dah de dah
We all know frogs go
Lod de dah de dah
They don't go gink gank gunk

Hiss Hiss went a little green snake one day
Hiss Hiss went a little green snake
Hiss Hiss went a little green snake one day
And his tail went rattle dattle do

But we know snakes go
Lod de dah de dah
Lod de dah de dah
Lod de dah de dah
We all know snakes go
Lod de dah de dah
They don't go rattle dattle do

Flap flap went the little green bird one day
Flap flap went the little green bird
Flap flap went the little green bird one day
And his song went tweet tweet tweet

But we know birds go
Lod de dah de dah
Lod de dah de dah
Lod de dah de dah
We all know birds go
Lod de dah de dah
They don't go tweet tweet tweet

Turning Phrases into Sentences

Lesson 20

Timed Activity (One Minute)

Instructor: *I am going to give you three words. I want you to use them in a good sentence or good sentences that make sense. The three words must be together in your sentence.*

Examples: three little pigs   **Three little pigs** were playing in the mud.

the oldest boy   Sam is **the oldest boy** in the class.

1. the old car
2. the hot fire
3. nice stranger
4. was very silly
5. reading and writing
6. spaghetti and meatballs
7. aunts and uncles
8. my best friend

Developing Expressive Language

Language Activity 20

1. Tell me some kinds of cars. What color car would you like? Would you rather fly in a plane or ride in a car?

2. What is dangerous about a hot fire? Where are some places we find hot fires?

3. Why do we not talk to strangers even if they seem nice? What are some tricks bad guys can use to get children to come to them?

4. Name something very silly. Name something very sad.

5. Why do we learn reading and writing? What would the world be like if there were no books?

6. What are some things you can do with a meatball? What are some things you should not do with a meatball?

7. Where would be the best place to meet all your aunts and uncles? What would you do if all your relatives were together at the same place and the same time?

8. What would you like to do with your best friend?

Vocabulary Building

Lesson 20

Tomato

Instructor: *What is red, round, has seeds, and you get a slice on your hamburger, if it's all the way? Yes, a tomato! I want you to think quietly about tomatoes and then raise your hand to give me a word to tell me something you know about them. It can be the color, their appearance, where you can find them, what can we make with them and so forth.*

What are some things you can think of that have tomatoes as a major ingredient?

There are many different kinds and sizes of tomatoes. Name some of the kinds you have seen at home or at the grocery store.

What are some kinds of foods that need tomatoes to make them better?

How do tomatoes grow?

Catsup is made from tomatoes. What do you like to put catsup on?

Developing Expressive Language

Singing

If You're Happy and You Know It

(American Children's Song with Latvian Origins)

If you're happy and you know it, clap your hands.

If you're happy and you know it, clap your hands.

If you're happy and you know it, then your face will surely show it.

If you're happy and you know it, clap your hands.

If you're happy and you know it, stamp your feet.

If you're happy and you know it, stamp your feet.

If you're happy and you know it, then your face will surely show it.

If you're happy and you know it, stamp your feet.

If you're happy and you know it, shout, "Whoopee!"

If you're happy and you know it, shout, "Whoopee!"

If you're happy and you know it, then your face will surely show it.

If you're happy and you know it, shout, "Whoopee!"

If you're happy and you know it, do all three!

If you're happy and you know it, do all three!

If you're happy and you know it, then your face will surely show it.

If you're happy and you know it, do all three!

Section III

Rhyming

Section III

Rhyming

Rhyming may very well be the most important skill to be developed in phonemic awareness. Rhyming helps our children understand "rimes", which are the sounds that letters make within words. When we chunk a group of sounds together as in the word "space", "ace" is a rime. When I put two words together as in "space race" I have a rhyme. With repeated experiences in rhyming, children gain a critical language sense that is invaluable in their later work with the written word. Many, if not most, researchers believe that it may be impossible to master reading without recognizing rime. We know for sure that the early learning of nursery rhymes and silly songs enhance reading skills and phonemic awareness.

It is important to remember that rhyming may very well be a developmental skill that emerges over time. Children master rhyming at different times in their language development. If there are difficulties, be patient with the students as they grow. Rhyming and understanding rhyming is gained through considerable practice and language facility. *Great Leaps* has many lessons and activities designed to bring students to proficiency in rhyming. However, if a student has persistent difficulty with rhyming, consider having the hearing screened. You may wish to talk to others involved with the child to see if they have noticed or think there could be hearing difficulties.

The lessons in this section should not take longer than one week each. We move on and keep practicing and learning because of the developmental issues involved. If you are working one on one with a child, you have more options as to movement. Be keenly aware of avoiding frustration and failure while working with these activities.

Remember, we do not stay longer than one week when we are working with groups in the rhyming activities.

Rhyming

Lesson 21 (One Minute)

Timed Activity

Instructor: *I am going to give you a word. I want you to tell me a word that sounds like the word I give you. I can give you a hint if you need it.*

Example: I am going to want a word that rhymes or sounds like sick. If you cannot come up with any, I will give you hints. With sick:

If you made a "t" sound you would get …. tick

If you make a "k" sound and you would get get … kick

What would you get if I gave you the br sound? Br with an ick.   Brick

In one minute we are going to see how many words can you get to rhyme with cow? I will wait for you to come up with one for five seconds. I'm going to give you ten seconds before we start to organize yourself and get ready. Then, I'll give a hint. (Mastery is five rhyming words in one minute.)

When you give me a correct rhyme, name another as soon as you can. If there are problems, I'll give you another hint.

Tell me as many words as you can that rhyme with cow.

Hint

B	bow
Br	brow
Ch	chow
H	how
N	now
P	pow
Pl	plow
S	sow
W	wow

Building Vocabulary

Lesson 21

Onion

Instructor: *Today's food is the onion. A long time ago, during the California Gold Rush, people called them skunk eggs. I want you to think quietly about onions for a minute and then raise your hand to give me a word to tell me something you know about them. It can be their color, what they look like, what they taste like, what they smell like, where you can find them, what do we do with them, and so forth.*

What are some different kinds of food that have onions in them?

How do onions grow?

What does an onion look like when you cut it open?

Why do you think some people cry when they cut an onion?

Why do you think the old California gold miners called onions "skunk eggs"?

Rhyming

Lesson 22

Instructor: *I am going to give you a hint. I want you to tell me a word that will answer the question and rhyme with the word flow.*

Example: Your answer is going to rhyme with flow. To put out a birthday candle you have to _____. Right! Blow. Blow rhymes with flow.

Are you ready? Remember, your answer must rhyme with flow or blow.

A girl can put this in her hair.	bow
This bird says "caw, caw."	crow
To toss a ball is to	throw
The desks in class are in a	row
The opposite of yes is	no
The opposite of high is	low
You do this with needle and thread.	Sew
You wiggle one of these inside your shoe.	Toe
On your mark, get set, …	Go
A boy or girls' name	Joe Moe Flo
What does a firefly do in the dark?	glow
The opposite of fast is	slow
When you get bigger you	grow

Developing Expressive Language
Mother Goose

Jack and Jill went up the hill,

To fetch a pail of water;

Jack fell down, and broke his crown,

And Jill came tumbling after.

Discussion: *Why do you think they had to go up the hill to get water? If you tripped and fell down a hill, what do you think would happen? It said that Jack broke his crown. What do you think he broke?*

Old King Cole was a merry old soul,

And a merry old soul was he;

He called for his pipe and he called for his bowl,

And he called for his fiddlers three.

Discussion: *Why do you think Old King Cole was so happy? Besides smoking his pipe and listening to music, what else do you think he would like? If you could have three musicians come and play music for you, which instruments would they be playing?*

Little Bo-peep has lost her sheep,

And can't tell where to find them;

Leave them alone, and they'll come home,

Wagging their tails behind them.

Discussion: *What is the advice for Little Bo Peep in the story? Do you think by doing nothing the sheep will come back home? What should she be doing? What are some chores you are expected to do at home?*

Building Vocabulary

Lesson 22

Bread

Instructor: *Today's food is bread. When you think about it, there are many kinds of bread. I want you to think quietly about bread and then be ready to talk about it. It can be the color, what it looks like, where you can find it, what do we do with it, and so forth.*

What different kinds of bread can you get at a bakery?

How do they cook the bread?

What is break made out of?

What all can you put on bread?

Developing Expressive Language

Singing

I'm a Little Teapot

I'm a little teapot
short and stout
Here is my handle
here is my spout

When I get all steamed up
Hear me shout
Just tip me over and pour me out!

© 1939 George Harold Sanders and Clarence C. Kelley

When you view this song from your search engine, note the action and movement that goes along with the song and teach it to the students.

Rhyming

Lesson 23

Timed Activity (One Minute)

Instructor: *I am going to give you a sound. I want you to tell me three words that sound like the sound that I give you. After five seconds I'll help. (Mastery is 12 words per minute)*

Example: I want three words that sound like "uff". If you can do more, that's great. Okay, give it a try.

buff   bluff   cuff   enough   fluff   gruff   huff   puff   rough   tough

Now, we can begin. Are you ready?

1. I want four words that rhyme with "it".

bit fit mitt lit kit knit pit quit zit hit

2. Four words that rhyme with "fly".

bye cry die dry dye fly fry guy high lie my pry shy sky sty tie try why

3. Four words that rhyme with "Sam".

am bam cam clam cram dam gram ham jam lamb Pam ram sham slam

If the student or class finishes the Sam rhymes before the minute is completed, go back to number one and continue.

Developing Expressive Language

Mother Goose

Little Jack Horner sat in a corner,

eating his Christmas pie.

He stuck in his thumb and pulled out a plum,

And said, "What a good boy am I!"

Discussion: What is going on here? What kind of pie do you think Jack Horner was eating? If you stuck your thumb in your favorite pie, is there anything you think you would pull out? What kind of pie would you like at Christmas?

Sing a song of sixpence, a pocket full of rye

Four and twenty blackbirds baked in a pie

When the pie was opened, the birds began to sing

Wasn't that a dainty dish to set before the king?

The king was in his counting-house counting out his money

The queen was in the parlor eating bread and honey

The maid was in the garden hanging out the clothes

When along came a blackbird and pecked off her nose.

Discussion: What is so silly about this Mother Goose rhyme? What are some things that could not ever really happen? Can someone really bake blackbirds in a pie? Why not?

Developing Expressive Language

Mother Goose

Baa, baa black sheep, Have you any wool?

Yes sir, yes sir, three bags full;

One for my master, one for my dame

and one for the little boy that lives in our lane.

Baa, baa black sheep, Have you any wool?

Discussion: What are sheep? What is wool? Why would the child in the story give a bag of wool to the little boy who lives on their street?

Hey! Diddle, Diddle, the cat and the fiddle

The cow jumped over the moon

The little dog laughed, to see such sport

And the dish ran away with the spoon!

Discussion: What is going on here? Why can't a cow jump over the moon? What could really make a dog laugh? So, with whom would a fork run away?

Developing Expressive Language

Singing

Hey, Ho Nobody Home
(Traditional English Round)

Hey, Ho Nobody Home
Eat, nor Drink, nor Money
Have I none.
Yet, I will be
Me – er- er – ry
Hey, Ho Nobody Home

Note: This is an opportunity to teach the children how to sing the song as a round.

Rhyming

Lesson 24

Timed Activity (One Minute)

Instructor: *I am going to give you a word with an ending sound. I want you to tell me some words that sound like or rhyme with the word I give you. After five seconds I'll help.*

Example: I want three words that sound like "ite". If you can do more, that's great.

bite delight fight flight fright height kite light might night polite quite night

Now, your turn:

1. I want four words that rhyme with "ink."

blink clink drink fink link mink pink rink slink stink wink

2. Four words that rhyme with "fly".

by cry die dry dye fly fry guy high lie my pry shy sky sty tie try why

3. Four or more words that rhyme with "oat".

boat coat float goat gloat moat note quote throat wrote

(Note: if the student finishes the exercise in less than a minute, you send them back up to the top to continue.)

Developing Expressive Language

Singing

Take Me Out to the Ballgame
©1908 Jack Norworth and Albert von Tilzer

Take me out to the ball game,

Take me out with the crowd;

Buy me some peanuts and Cracker Jacks,

I don't care if I never get back.

For it's root, root, root for the home team,

If they don't win, it's a shame.

For it's one,

two,

three strikes, you're out,

At the old ball game.

Rhyming

Lesson 25

Timed Activity (One Minute)

Instructor: *We can rhyme to a given category. An example would be in the rhyming of names: Sam and Pam or Bill and Phil or Jill. If you cannot come up with an answer, I'll give you the first sound.*

Practice: Can you tell me a rhyming name for Stan?

Let's try Jim. (See if the student can do this, if not, help).

Now, let's begin.

1. Give me two names that rhyme with Rick? (Nick, Vic, Mick, Slick)

2. Give me two names that rhyme with Drew? (Sue, Hugh, Lou)

3. Two names that rhyme with John? (Ron, Don, Lon, Tron, Sean)

4. Two names that rhyme with Ronnie? (Johnnie, Donny, Connie, Bonnie)

*The goal here is eight words rhyming in one minute. If the students get their eight words and finish with **Ronnie**, then go back up to **Rick** to continue. When the minute is up,, the activity is over.*

The children now should be learning the previous songs, and hopefully having fun with them. Though we add songs as an activity, do not hesitate to have fun and sing more than one.

Developing Expressive Language

Singing

I'm Henery the Eighth, I Am
English Folk Song

I'm Henery the Eighth, I am,
Henery the Eighth I am, I am!
I got married to the widow next door,
She's been married seven times before.
And every one was an Henery
It wouldn't be a Willie or a Sam
  I'm her eighth old man I'm Henery
Henery the Eighth, I am!

Second verse, same as the first!
I'm Henery ….

©1910 Fred Murray and R. P. Weston

Rhyming

Lesson 26

Timed Activity (One Minute)

Rhyming words sound alike. Here are two examples of rhyming names:

    Sam and Pam   or   Bill and Phil or Jill.

Practice: Can you tell me a rhyming name for Stan? *(Help if needed. Always give time for thought.)*

    Let's try Jim.

Now, let's begin. Are you comfortable and ready? Begin. *(begin the timer)*

1. Can you give me two names that rhyme with Mary? (Kerry, Harry, Gary)

2. Can you give me two names that rhyme with Ken? (Ben, Jen, Sven)

3. Two names that rhyme with Minnie? (Benny, Denny, Jenny)

4. Two names that rhyme with Ann?   (Dan, Fran, Jan, Nan, Stan)

The goal here is 8. If the child finishes the two Ann rhymes, you go back to number one. You will note that ELL students will have particular difficulty in many of the rhyming activities. This takes time to master. Avoid frustration by giving examples and help.

Developing Expressive Language

Singing

Knick Knack
Welsh Folk Song

This old man, he played one,
He played knick-knack on my thumb.
With a knick-knack, paddy whack,
Give a dog a bone,
This old man came rolling home.

This old man, he played two,
He played knick-knack on my shoe.
With a knick-knack, paddy whack,
Give a dog a bone,
This old man came rolling home.

This old man, he played three,
He played knick-knack on my knee.
With a knick-knack, paddy whack,
Give a dog a bone,
This old man came rolling home.

This old man, he played four,
He played knick-knack on my door.
With a knick-knack, paddy whack,
Give a dog a bone,
This old man came rolling home.

This old man, he played five,
He played knick-knack on my hive.
With a knick-knack, paddy whack,
Give a dog a bone,
This old man came rolling home.

This old man, he played six,
He played knick-knack on my sticks.
With a knick-knack, paddy whack,
Give a dog a bone,
This old man came rolling home.

This old man, he played seven,
He played knick-knack up in heaven.
With a knick-knack, paddy whack,
Give a dog a bone,
This old man came rolling home.

This old man, he played eight,
He played knick-knack on my gate.
With a knick-knack, paddy whack,
Give a dog a bone,
This old man came rolling home.

This old man, he played nine.
He played knick-knack on my spine.
With a knick-knack, paddy whack,
Give a dog a bone.
This old man came rolling home.

This old man, he played ten.
He played knick-knack once again.
With a knick-knack, paddy whack,
Give a dog a bone.
The last old man came rolling home.

Note: Use the search engine to view the actions that go with the song.

Rhyming

Lesson 27

Timed Activity (One Minute)

Instructor: *I am going to give you the name of a color. I want you to tell me something that color that rhymes with the name of that color. (With a large group just have the kids wait two seconds and then call out answers. The instructor acknowledges the correct answers by repeating them like this, "Yes a yellow fellow is a good one." The answers must come with two words.)*

If the student is not getting the hang of thinking and rhyming at this point, you should realize that extra work outside the scope of Great Leaps may be required.

Example: If I said "red" you could say "red bed" or "red sled".

Practice: Can you give me something green? (green bean, green teen, green sheen,)

Ready?

1. How about something brown? (clown, crown, town, gown)

2. How about something blue? (brew, clue, goo, gnu, crew, dew, shoe)

3. Something black? (placque, sack, track, Jack, rack, shack)

4. Something white? (kite, light, knight)

5. Something pink? (mink, sink, skink, drink)

6. Something tan? (man, fan, can, van)

Developing Expressive Language

Singing

Miss Mary Mack
American Folk Clapping Song

Miss Mary Mack, Mack,
    All dressed in black, black, black,
with silver buttons, buttons, buttons,
    All down her back, back, back.
She asked her mother, mother, mother,
    For 50 cents, cents, cents,
to see the elephants, elephants, elephants,
    Jump over the fence, fence, fence.
They jumped so high, high, high,
    they reached the sky, sky, sky
They jumped so low, low, low
    They stubbed their toe, toe, toe
and they didn't come back, back, back,
    'Til the 4th of July, ly, ly!
And now we play, play, play.
    All night and day, day, day
With Mary Mack, Mack, Mack
    on the railroad track track track.

To get the tune, go to a search engine and put in "Miss Mary Mack." You can also look up "the Name Game"

Rhyming

Lesson 28

Timed Activity (One Minute)

Instructor: *Do these words rhyme? Answer yes or no.*
Let's practice. (freak, lake) No, they do not rhyme.
One more. (flea, tree) Yes, these rhyme.
Ready?

1. rake, flake   (yes)
2. beak, snake   (no)
3. thing, sting   (yes)
4. grime, slime   (yes)
5. monkey, funky   (yes)
6. trail, trial   (no)
7. cling, clang   (no)
8. brought, fought   (yes)
9. carrot, basketball (no)
10. funny, money   (yes)
11. sleepy, creepy   (yes)
12. icky, bug   (no)

Developing Expressive Language

Singing

It's Raining
English Folk Song

It's raining, it's pouring;   The old man is snoring.

He went to bed and he bumped his head

And he couldn't get up in the morning.

Rain, rain go away, we want to go out and play.

It's storming. It's howling.

The old man is scowling.

  He wants to eat, but there is no meat

and his belly is growling.

Storm, storm go away, we want to go out and play.

It's comfy and sunny.

The old man has money.

He had to sneeze around a bunch of bees

and they didn't find it funny.

Rain, rain stay away

We want to stay outside and play.

Words modified by Kenneth U. Campbell (2013)

Rhyming

Lesson 29

Timed Activity (One Minute)

Instructor: *Do these words rhyme? Answer yes or no. Let's practice. (most, host) Yes, they rhyme. One more. (bear, boar) No, they do not rhyme. Ready?*

1.	racket, packet	(yes)
2.	motor, silver	(no)
3.	monster, master	(no)
4.	copy, sloppy	(yes)
5.	stupider, Jupiter	(yes)
6.	girls, grills	(no)
7.	sloppy, floppy	(yes)
8.	throat, float	(yes)
9.	snake, dinosaur	(no)
10.	sleeping, typing	(no)
11.	hound dog, bullfrog	(yes)
12.	crocodile, walk a mile	(yes)

Developing Expressive Language

Singing

Pop Goes the Weasel
English Folk Song

Round and round the cobbler's bench,

the monkey chased the weasel.

The monkey thought it was all for fun.

Pop! Goes the weasel.

A penny for a spool of thread, a penny for a needle;

that's the way the money goes,

Pop! Goes the weasel.

All around the mulberry bush

The monkey chased the weasel

The monkey thought it was all in sport

Pop! Goes the weasel.

A penny for a spool of thread, a penny for a needle,

that's the way the money goes,

Pop! Goes the weasel.

Rhyming

Lesson 30

Timed Activity (One Minute)

Instructor: *Which of the three words does not rhyme? (watch my lips) If you do not know what the word means, at the end please ask me and I'll tell you.*

Example: red, mad, sled (Mad does not rhyme)

Practice: bell Bill Phil (Bell does not rhyme)

Ready?

Which of these three words does not rhyme?

1. my   slow   tie   (slow)
2. funny   honey   bean   (bean)
3. trick   silly   hilly   (trick)
4. blue   few   mill   (mill)
5. stick   book   hook   (stick)
6. slime   slow   crime   (slow)
7. slight tight   strong   (strong)
8   four   send   friend   (four)
9. may   might   night   (may)
10. gray   hay   horse   (horse)
11. green   grass   scene   (grass)
12. road   frog   log   (road)

Developing Expressive Language

Singing

Over the River and Through the Wood
1844 - Lydia Mary Child

Over the river and through the wood
to Grandmother's house we go.
The horse knows the way to carry the sleigh
Through the white and drifted snow, oh!

Over the river and through the wood,
Oh, how fast the wind does blow.
It stings my toes and bites my nose
As over the ground we go.

Note: Students could draw a picture of what the see in this song.

Rhyming

Timed Activity (One Minute)

Lesson 31

Instructor: *Which of the three words does not rhyme? (watch my lips) If you do not know what the word means, at the end please ask me and I'll tell you.*

Example: red, mad, sled (Mad does not rhyme)

Practice: bell Bill Phil (Bell does not rhyme)

Ready to begin? Okay, I'm starting the timer.

Which of these three does not rhyme?

1. great freak eight (freak)
2. happy money honey (happy)
3. treat trap feet (trap)
4. rust trust mast (mast)
5. climb mine rhyme (mine)
6. pauper paper taper (pauper)
7. dim brown clown (dim)
8. fluster mister blister (fluster)
9. crimp camp clamp (crimp)
10. truck trick duck (trick)
11. road toad toast (toast)
12. feeling, trusting, healing (trusting)

Expressive Language Development

Singing

Cinderella Dressed in Yella
American Jump Rope Song

Cinderella dressed in yella; went upstairs to kiss her fella.
By mistake she kissed a snake. How many doctors will it take?

(point to a student who will then name the number and everyone in unison claps as they count)

1, 2, 3, 4, 5, 6, 7, 8, 9, etc.

Cinderella dressed in blue, went upstairs to tie her shoe. Made a mistake and tied a knot. How many knots will she make?

1, 2, 3, 4, 5, 6, 7, 8, 9, etc.

Cinderella dressed in green, went downtown to buy a wedding ring. Made a mistake and bought a fake. How many days before it breaks?

1, 2, 3, 4, 5, 6, 7, 8, 9, etc.

In this activity a student chooses a number from one to ten and the group claps that number.

Rhyming

Lesson 32 (Untimed)

Instructor: *Two of the three words rhyme. Which ones are they?*

Example: red, mad, sled   (Red and sled rhyme)

Practice: bell, Bill, Phil   (Bill and Phil rhyme)

Ready?

Say the two words that rhyme.

1. great freak eight   (great and eight)
2. happy money honey   (money and honey)
3. treat trap feet   (treat and feet)
4. rust trust mast   (rust and trust)
5. climb mine rhyme   (climb and rhyme)
6. pauper paper taper   (paper and taper)
7. dim brown clown   (brown and clown)
8. fluster mister blister   (mister and blister)
9. crimp camp clamp   (camp and clamp)
10. truck trick duck   (truck and duck)
11. road toad toast   (road and toad)
12. feeling, trusting, healing (feeling and healing)

Developing Expressive Language

Singing

The Ants Go Marching
American Children's Song, Author Unknown

1. The ants go marching one by one,
   hurrah, hurrah
   The ants go marching one by one,
   hurrah, hurrah
   The ants go marching one by one,
   The little one stops to suck his thumb
   And they all go marching down to the ground
   To get out of the rain,
   boom boom boom boom   boom boom bom boom

2. The ants go marching two by two,
   The little one stops to tie his shoe

3. The little one stops to climb a tree
   And they all go marching down to the ground

4. The little one stops to shut the door
   And they all go marching down to the ground

5. The little one stops to take a dive
   And they all go marching down to the ground

6. The little one stops to pick up sticks
   And they all go marching down to the ground

7. The little one stops to ask a question
   And they all go marching down to the ground

8. The little one stops to shut the gate
   And they all go marching down to the ground

9. The little one stops to check the time
   And they all go marching down to the ground

10. The little one stops to say "THE END"
    And they all go marching down to the ground
    To get out of the rain
    boom boom boom boom   boom boom bom boom

Section IV

Phonemic Awareness

Phonemic Awareness

Phonemic awareness is one part of phonological awareness. Phonological awareness is the detection and manipulation of sounds. Phonemic awareness is more specific, it is where listeners are able to hear, identify and manipulate phonemes.

When coupled with phonics instruction, this has been called the "code" of reading. When students have been taught and understand "the code" they are on their way to becoming independent readers. These skills are also integral to good spelling and eventually writing.

Beginning Sounds

Lesson 33

Timed Activity (One Minute)

Instructor: *Tell me the beginning sound of: coat   (k)*

Practice Two: Tell me the beginning sound of master: (m)

Ready?

1. Tell me the beginning sound   of :   finger (f)
2. of: dinosaur (d)
3. of: bite   (b)
4. of: go   (g)
5. of: pink   (p)
6. of: pimple (p)
7. of: monster (m)
8. of: jet (j)
9. of: teacher (t)
10. of: road (r)
11. of: book (b)
12. of: zoo (z)
13. of: vessel (v)
14. of: hurricane (h)
15. of: Cyclops (s)

Developing Expressive Language

Singing

I've Been Working on the Railroad
American Folk Song

I've been working on the railroad
All the live-long day.
I've been working on the railroad
Just to pass the time away.
Can't you hear the whistle blowing,
Rise up so early in the morn;
Can't you hear the captain shouting,
"Dinah, blow your horn!"

Dinah, won't you blow,
Dinah, won't you blow,
Dinah, won't you blow your horn?
Dinah, won't you blow,
Dinah, won't you blow,
Dinah, won't you blow your horn?

Someone's in the kitchen with Dinah
Someone's in the kitchen I know
Someone's in the kitchen with Dinah
Strummin' on the old banjo!

And singin' fee, fie, fiddly-i-o
Fee, fie, fiddly-i-o-o-o-o
Fee, fie, fiddly-i-o
Strummin' on the old banjo.

Strummin' on the old banjo!

Ending Sounds

Lesson 34

Timed Activity (One Minute)

Instructor: T*ell me the ending sound of: flight (t)*

Practice Two: tell me the ending sound of rough: (f)

Ready?

1. Tell me the ending sound   of :   blame (m)
2.   of: course (s)
3.   of: flip (p)
4.   of: bingo (o)
5.   of: werewolf (f)
6.   of: toast (t)
7.   of: train (n)
8.   of: bike (k)
9.   of: slip (p)
10.   of: cookie (e)
11.   of: French fries (s or z)
12.   of: rug (g)
13.   of: alibi (i)
14.   of: past (t)
15.   of: bash (sh)

Developing Expressive Language

Singing

IF I HAD A HAMMER (The Hammer Song)
words and music by Lee Hays and Pete Seeger

This is a fantastic song for children who have been in the habit of singing for a few months. The organization of the lyrics and the positive message are truly motivational. There are many great versions of this song that can be found online.

Beginning Sounds

Lesson 35 (One Minute)

Timed Activity

Instructor: *Which two words have the same beginning sound?*

Example: plane bus plus   *(Plane and plus both have the "pl" beginning)*

You try a one: drink drip bark   *(drink and drip)*

Ready?

1. staff bubble boat   (bubble and boat)
2. throw that thrust   (throw and thrust)
3. task tusk dusk   (task and tusk)
4. flip frighten fresh   (frighten and fresh)
5. stamp risk study   (stamp and study)
6. hurry grapes grin   (grapes and grin)
7. church chimp shrimp   (church and chimp)
8. duke king kiss   (king and kiss)
9. crust climb crab   (crust and crab)
10. paper quake person   (paper and person)
11. spleen green grapes   (green and grapes)
12. touchdown field tap   (touchdown and tap)

Developing Expressive Language

Singing

A Sailor Went to Sea
(British Folk Song)

A sailor went to sea, sea, sea,
To see what he could see, see, see,
And all that he could see, see, see,
Was the bottom of the deep blue sea, sea, sea!

A sailor went to chop, chop, chop,
To see what he could chop, chop, chop,
And all that he could chop, chop, chop,
Was the bottom of the deep blue chop, chop, chop!

A sailor went to knee, knee, knee,
To see what he could knee, knee, knee,
And all that he could knee, knee, knee,
Was the bottom of the deep blue knee, knee, knee!

The sailor went to sea, chop, knee,
To see what he could sea, chop, knee,
And all that he could sea, chop, ,knee,
Was the bottom of the deep blue sea, chop, knee!

Note and reminder: use your search engine to discover the tunes and any student activities that not only go with this song, but with all the songs in Great Leaps.

Working with Beginning Sounds

Lesson 36

Timed Activity (One Minute)

Instructor: *Example: Tell me two words that begin with "gr". green and grape*

Now you try one. Tell me two words that begin with "fl".

Tell me two words that begin with "sp".

Ready?

1. Tell me two words that begin with "tr". (train, trip, triple, trend, trap, trust)
2. that begin with "cl". (club, climb, clam, clamp, class)
3. that begin with "bl". (blue, black, blister, blink, blast)
4. that begin with "st". (stamp, store, stump, stick)
5. that begin with "ch". (chimp, champ, chump, church)
6. that begin with "sh". (shirt, shampoo, sugar, shop)
7. that begin with "gl". (glue, glass, globe, gleem, glee)
8. that begin with "pr". (pride, prune, print, prey, president)
9. that begin with "qu". (queen, quick, quack, quit, quiet)
10. that begin with "br". (brick, brag, bring, bread, brat)

Developing Expressive Language

Singing

Tiny Tim the Turtle
(American Children's Folk Song)

I had a little turtle,
his name was Tiny Tim.
I put him in the bathtub,
to see if he could swim.

He drank up all the water,
he ate up all the soap,
Tiny Tim was choking
on the bubbles in his throat.

In came the doctor,
in came the nurse,
in came the lady,
with the alligator purse.

They pumped out all the water.
They pumped out all the soap.
They popped the airy bubbles
as they floated from his throat.

Out went the doctor,
out went the nurse,
out went the lady,
with the alligator purse.

Alliteration

Lesson 37

Timed Activity (One Minute)

Instructor: *Which two words in the sentence have the same beginning sound? Hint: in this lesson they will be right by each other.*

Example: She has really red hair. (Really and red have the "r" sound.

Now you try one.

It is really raining. (really and raining begin with the "r" sound.

One more practice: That is sour soup. (sour and soup begin with the "s" sound.

Now, let's see if we can do five in a minute or less. Can we find more than five?

1. We do jumping jacks for exercise. (jumping jacks begin with the "j" sound.)

2. Dirty Dan will not be allowed on the field trip. (Dirty and Dan begin with the "d" sound.)

3. I ate four french-fries. (Four french-fries begin with the "f" sound.)

4. Boy, is that a pretty picture. (Pretty and picture begin with the "P" sound.)

5. That is a chewy chocolate candy bar. (Chewy and chocolate begin the "ch" sound.)

6. We're having a late lunch. (Late and lunch begin with the "l" sound.)

7. She believes she is a pretty princess. (Pretty and Princess begin with the "pr" sound.)

8. Billy Bird lives on Third. (Billy and Bird both begin with the "b" sound.)

9. Look at that crabby crawdad. (crabby and crawdad both begin with the "cr" sound.)

10. Yuck, I don't like peppery popcorn. (peppery and popcorn both begin with the "p" sound.)

Developing Expressive Language

Singing

Billy Goat Hide and Seek
(African American Folk Song)

I went down the road, the road was muddy.

Stubbed my toe, the toe was bloody.

Can you all hear? Yell, "Billy Goat!"

If you're not hid, the boat won't float.

Five, ten, fifteen, twenty

twenty-five, thirty, thirty-five, forty

Can you all hear? Yell, "Billy Goat!"

If you're not hid, the boat won't float.

Mamma in the garden, Daddy's gone fishin'

I'm sittin' on a tree stump wishin'

Mamma get strawberries, Daddy catch bream

Then we'll be eatin' like Tiny Tim!

Can you all hear? Yell, "Billy Goat!"

If you're not hid, the boat won't float.

Crawdaddy stew and pumpkin pie

I know full well that a snake can't fly

Cause if he could, he'd bite my head

And that would make all my hair turn red

Can you all hear? Yell, "Billy Goat!"

If you're not hid, the boat won't float.

Two dirty kids only one bar of soap

It don't need fixin' if it ain't broke

Scrub it with bubbles from head to toe

And if that don't do it, gotta scrub some more.

Can you all hear? Yell, "Billy Goat!"

If you're not hid, the boat won't float.

One potato, two potato, three potato, four

You gotta be ready cause here I go

And if you ain't hid, it's now too late

Cause here I come, and I can't wait.

African American children's hide and seek song. Lyrics updated by Kenneth U. Campbell (2013). For the basic tune websearch "Hide and seek billy goat."

Alliteration

Lesson 38

Timed Activity (One Minute)

Instructor: *This exercise is a like the one where you had to find which two words in the sentence had the same beginning sound. Now, I'm going to ask you to make up a sentence where two words that are by each other have the same beginning sound.*

Example: Like this. I give the sound (p). I want to go to a pumpkin party. Or -

Look at that pink poodle. Or - I am a proud parent.

Practice: Can you do one?

Now try it with the sound "s".

Are you ready to do them with the timer on? Okay, I'm going to give you the sound and I want you to tell me a sentence that puts two words together with that sound. Five is a goal

1. The sound "L" (I see a loud lion.)
2. The sound "B" (I love beef burritos.)
3. The sound "M" (I need more money.)
4. The sound short "A" (I ran after alligators.)
5. The sound "R" (There goes Road Runner.)
6. The sound "F" (I saw a fat fox.)
7. The sound "T" (There are two trucks.)

Developing Expressive Language
Singing

Engine, Engine Number Nine (Amercian Folk Song)

Engine, engine number nine. Running down the New York line. I will bring an empty plate, because their pizza is so great.

Engine, engine number nine. Running down Miami line; running east, running west. Running through the cuckoo's nest.

Engine, engine number nine, running down the L.A. line.

When I stop and I look back, I see monkeys on the track

Others

London – if we happen to meet the Queen, would you give her something green

Paris – if we hear the dinner bells, will they make us all eat snails

New Orleans – The tracks are wet and very slippy, is that really the Mississippi

Cairo – if we make the daddy sad, will that make the mummy mad

Tokyo - if we hear the old crow caw, must we eat that sushi raw

Atlanta – If we go eat at the Ritz, will they serve us all cheese grits

Mumbai – if you hear your britches rip, I think it's time to end this trip

Consonant Blends

Lesson 39

Timed Activity (One Minute)

Instructor: *This exercise is a lot like the one where you had to find which two words in the sentence had the same beginning sound. Now, I'm going to ask you to make up a sentence where two words that are by each other have the same beginning blending sound.*

Example: I give the sound (pl). Look at those plastic plates. Or -

That is Pluto's place.

Practice: Can you do one?

Now try it with the sound "st".

Are you ready to do these with the timer on? Okay, I'm going to give you the sound and I want you to tell me a sentence that puts two words together with that sound. Five is a goal.

1. The sound "br"   (bring breakfast, brass bricks, broken brains)
2. The sound "sl"   (slick slime, slippery slide, slow sled)
3. The sound "cr"   (crisp cracker, creepy crow, cracked crayons)
4. The sound "cl"   (class clown, close cloud, climbing club)
5. The sound "gr"   (great grin, grabbing grapes, growing greens)

The instructor may have many teaching opportunities before the students get this one. This can be very silly and fun. The class can brainstorm, with the instructor modeling how you go through the alphabet looking in your mind for the good combos.

Developing Expressive Language

Singing

Old Folks at Home (Suwanee River)
Stephen Foster, 1851

Way down upon the Suwanee River,

Far, far away,

There's where my heart is turning ever,

There's where the old folks stay.

All up and down the whole creation

Sadly I roam,

Still longing for the old plantation,

And for the old folks at home.

All the world is sad and dreary,

Everywhere I roam;

Oh, how my heart grows sad and weary,

Far from the old folks at home!

This is the official state song of Florida.

Ending Sounds

Lesson 40

Timed Activity (One Minute)

Instructor: *Listen as I say a word. Then I will say it again but leave off its ending sound. Tell me what sound I left out. Not the entire word, just the sound I left out.*

Example: freak …. frea ….. Right, I left out the "k" sound.

Now you try a couple: brother …. broth …   (er)

airplane …. airpl…   (ane)

1. barn ….. bar   (n)
2. sneeze …. snee   (z)
3. town …. tow   (n)
4. frighten …. fright   (en)
5. surfing …. surf   (ing)
6. pineapple … pineapp   (le)
7. clock …. clo   (k)
8. box… bo   (x)
9. teeth … tee   (th)
10. tongue … ton   (g)

Developing Expressive Language

Singing

She Threw it Out the Window
(American Scouting Song)

Old Mother Hubbard went to the cupboard

To fetch her poor dog a bone

But when she got there the cupboard was bare

So she threw it out the window

(Chorus:) The window, the window, the second-story window.

But when she got there, the cupboard was bare

(Note: always the 3rd line of the previous verse)

So she threw it out the window

Old King Cole was a merry old soul

And a merry old soul was he

He called for his pipe and he called for his bowl

And he threw them out the window   (Chorus)

Yankee Doodle went to town A-riding on a pony

He stuck a feather in his cap And threw it out...   (Chorus)

(Note: Any nursery rhyme can be added into this song.)

Using Contextual Clues

Lesson 41

Timed Activity (One Minute)

Instructor: *I am going to say a sentence but I will not finish the last word. I want you to finish the sentence with a word that makes sense.*

Example: We stopped at the railroad ___. (What are some possibilities of the missing word?)   tracks, warning sign

Now you try one. My mother has roses in her ___. garden, hair, vase

Ready?

1. One more than twenty-nine is ___.   (thirty)
2. I want to go to Disney ___.   (World, Land)
3. You cannot play basketball without a ___. (ball, court, net)
4. Have you ever been a passenger on a ___? (train, plane, bus)
5. Climb the very highest ___. (hill, mountain, tower)
6. If I went deep sea diving, I would be afraid of ___. (sharks, barracudas, drowning)
7. My favorite sandwich for lunch is a ___. (hamburger, cheese, ham)
8. The best way to get to England is by ___. (plane, ship, jet)
9. I love to go outside and play ___. (tag, chase, basketball)
10. More than anything, I would like a pet ___. (dog, cat, pony)

Developing Expressive Language
Singing

The Muffin Man
(English Folk Song)

Oh, do you know the muffin man,

The muffin man, the muffin man,

Oh, do you know the muffin man,

That lives on Drury Lane?

Oh, yes, I know the muffin man,

The muffin man, the muffin man,

Oh, yes, I know the muffin man,

That lives on Drury Lane.

Note: The instructor can make neat additions. Example: DO you know the donut man... he can live on whatever road you wish. Do you know the bus driver.. she lives on 42nd Street... etc.

Beginning Sounds

Lesson 42

Working with words through initial phonemes.

Timed Activity (One Minute)

Instructor: *I am going to give you a sound. Then, I am going to give you a clue as to a word that begins with that sound.*

Example: I am thinking of an animal, insect or bird that begins with the sound:

Sp – yes, spider.

You try one: L   (lion, lynx)

Okay – Let's see if you can get ten in a minute: Remember, we need the names of animals, insects or birds.

1. K (kangaroo, koala bear, cuckoo, cow)
2. M (monkey, manatee, mosquito, marlin)
3. R (rat, rabbit, wren, raccoon, rhino)
4. L (lion, lamb, lark. lizard)
5. D (dingo, deer, donkey, duck)
6. T (tiger, tadpole, toad, turtle)
7. F (frog, flea, fish, fox)
8. W (whale, wasp, wolf, walrus)
9. Ch (chimp, chicken, chipmunk, cheetah)
10. B (baboon, blacksnake, boa, buffalo)

Note: If number 10 gets finished and there is still time left, go back up to the top and continue. Ten in one minute is the goal.

Developing Expressive Language

Singing

Yankee Doodle
(American Folk Song)

Yankee Doodle went to town
A-riding on a pony,
Stuck a feather in his cap
And called it 'macaroni'.

Chorus:
Yankee Doodle keep it up,
Yankee Doodle dandy,
Mind the music and the step,
And with the girls be handy.

Beginning Sounds

Lesson 43

Timed Activity (One Minute)

Instructor: *I am going to give you a sound. Then, I am going to give you a clue as to a word that begins with that sound.*

Example: I am thinking of a vehicle, something that can be ridden, driven or flown – this includes brand names and types:

J – yes, Jeep, jet or Jaguar

You try one: T (Examples: truck, Trans-am, tricycle)

Okay – Let's see if you can get ten in a minute: (Examples are given for the instructor)

1. M (examples: motorcycle, Moped, mule, minivan)
2. P (plane, Plymouth, pony)
3. Tr (truck, tractor, train, tricycle)
4. S (skateboard, surfboard, skates, skooter)
5. B (bus, biplane, blimp, boat, bicycle)
6. C or K (Corvette, car, camel, convertible)
7. D (dumptruck, Dodge, dinghy, donkey)
8. Sh (Chevy, ship, showboat)
9. S (sled, surfboard, snow mobile skis, shuttle)
10. R (roller coaster, rickshaw, rocket, wrecker)

Developing Expressive Language

Singing

John Jacob Jingleheimer Schmidt
(American Folk Song)

John Jacob Jingleheimer Schmidt
His name is my name, too!
Whenever we go out,
The people always shout
There goes John Jacob Jingleheimer Schmidt!
Da da da da da da da

John Jacob Jingleheimer Schmidt
His name is my name, too!
Whenever we go out,
The people always shout
There goes John Jacob Jingleheimer Schmidt!
Da da da da da da da

John Jacob Jingleheimer Schmidt
His name is my name, too!
Whenever we go out,
The people always shout
There goes John Jacob Jingleheimer Schmidt!
Da da da da da da da

Sing the verse as many times as you like. Each time you sing the verse, sing a tad softer and then really shout "There goes John Jacob Jingleheimer Schmidt. There are many examples of this song that can be found with your search engine.

Beginning Sounds

Lesson 44

Timed Activity (One Minute)

Instructor: *I am going to give you a sound. Then, I am going to give you a clue as to a word that begins with that sound.*

Example: I am thinking of a game or toy that I can play with a friend..

M – yes, marbles or Monopoly

You try one: T (Examples: tag, touch football, t-ball)

Okay – Let's see if you can get ten in a minute: (Examples are given for the instructor)

1. F   (football, foosball, frizbee)
2. D   (doll, dodge ball, dominos)
3. S   (soccer, skating, Simon Says)
4. B   (Barbie, basketball, Bingo, bowling)
5. H   hide and seek, hopscotch, hacky sacks)
6. C or K   (catch, Clue, cards, kite, climbing)
7. M   (marbles, May I, Monopoly, magic)
8. P   (pogo stick, paper airplane, ping pong)
9. T   (trampoline, toy truck, tag)
10. R   (rubber ball, ring toss, rope)

Developing Expressive Language

Singing

The Grand Old Duke of York
(English Folk Song)

Oh, The grand old Duke of York,

He had ten thousand men;

He marched them up to the top of the hill,

And he marched them down again.

And when they were up, they were up,

And when they were down, they were down,

And when they were only half-way up,

They were neither up nor down.

This can be a fun activity song – children can march, go up, go down, etc.

Beginning Sounds

Lesson 45

Timed Activity (One Minute)

Instructor: *I am going to give you a sound. Then, I am going to give you a clue as to a word that begins with that sound.*

Example: I am thinking of something that can be eaten.

Ch – yes, chicken or chickpeas or cheese

You try one: T (Examples: turkey, tomatoes, Tootsie Roll, toast)

Okay – Let's see if you can get ten in a minute: (Examples are given for the instructor)

1. F   (examples: french-fries, fajitas, fish, fruit)
2. B   (bread, bananas, biscuits, burritos, bacon)
3. S   (squash, sushi, salt, sausage, sandwich, soup)
4. M   (macaroni and cheese, mashed potatoes, melon)
5. D   (dates, donuts, dip, Doritos)
6. C or K (cookies, crackers, crab cakes, coconut)
7. H   (hamburgers, hotdogs, hot sauce, ham)
8. P   (pudding, pizza, pickles, peanut butter)
9. Br   (bread, broccoli, brownies)
10. R   (raspberries, raisins, rice, roast beef, radishes)

Developing Expressive Language

Singing

This Little Light of Mine
Harry Dixon (1920)

This little light of mine I'm gonna let it shine

This little light of mine I'm gonna let it shine

This little light of mine I'm gonna let it shine

Let it shine Let it shine Let it shine

Everywhere I go I'm gonna let it shine

Everywhere I go I'm gonna let it shine

Everywhere I go I'm gonna let it shine

Let it shine Let it shine Let it shine

Hide it under a bushel Oh no!

I'm going to let it shine

Hide it under a bushel Oh no!

I'm going to let it shine

Hide it under a bushel Oh no!

I'm going to let it shine

Let it Shine All the time Let it shine!

Oh yeah!

Ending Sounds

Lesson 46

Timed Activity (One Minute)

Instructor: *I am going to tell you a word. I want you to repeat the word – but I want you to leave out the beginning sound.*

Example: If a say "puppy" then you'd say, "uppy"

Let's try two:

    Bank   ank

    Mother   other

Okay. Are you ready? Begin.

1. cat   at
2. ball   all
3. table   able
4. monkey   onkey
5. sick   ick
6. tall   all
7. chair   air
8. song   ong
9. girl   irl
10. baton   aton

Developing Expressive Language

Singing

Little Liza Jane
(African American Folk Song)

I got a gal that I adore

Little Liza Jane

Way down south in Baltimore

Little Liza Jane

Chorus: Oh Eliza, Little Liza Jane

Oh Eliza, Little Liza Jane

Down where she lives the posies grow

Little Liza Jane

Chickens round the kitchen door

Little Liza Jane

(Repeat Chorus)

I don't care how far we roam

Little Liza Jane

Where she's at is home sweet home

Little Liza Jane

(Repeat Chorus)

Ending Sounds

Lesson 47

Blends

Timed Activity (One Minute)

Instructor: *Example: If a say "brick" then you'd say, "ick"*

Let's try two:

    Sting   ing

    Train   ain

Okay. Are you ready? Begin.

1. fling   ing
2. flat   at
3. stop   op
4. grab   ab
5. grain   ain
6. store   ore
7. blink   ink
8. trick   ick
9. price   ice
10. clown   own

Developing Expressive Language

Singing

Clementine
(Folk Song of the American West)

In a cavern, in a canyon, excavating for a mine,

lived a miner, forty-niner, and his daughter Clementine.

> *Chorus: Oh my darling, Oh my darling, Oh my darling Clementine,*
>
> *You are lost and gone forever, dreadful sorry, Clementine.*

Light she was, and like a fairy, and her shoes were number nine,

Herring boxes without topses, sandals were for Clementine.

chorus

Drove she ducklings to the water every morning just at nine,

hit her foot against a splinter, fell into the foaming brine.

chorus

Ruby lips above the water, blowing bubbles soft and fine,

alas for me! I was no swimmer, so I lost my Clementine.

chorus

In a churchyard near the canyon, where the myrtle doth entwine,

There grow roses and other posies, fertilized by Clementine.

chorus

Then the miner, forty-niner, soon began to peak and pine,

Thought he oughter join his daughter, now he's with his Clementine.

chorus

In my dreams she still does haunt me, robed in garments soaked in brine,

while in life I used to hug her, now she's dead I draw the line.

chorus

Ending Sounds

Lesson 48

Timed Activity

Instructor: *I am going to say a word. I want you to repeat the word – but I want you to leave out the ending sound.*

Example: If I say "trick", I want you to say "tri"

Let's try two:

    Fruit …. Yes, "fru"

    Treat … Yes, "trea"

Okay. Are you ready? Begin.

1. plane   pla
2. shop   sho
3. radio   radi
4. clock   clo
5. fool   foo
6. phone   pho
7. write   wri
8. mouse   mou
9. glass   gla
10. tree   tr

Developing Expressive Language

Singing

When Johnnie Comes Marching Home
Patrick Gilmore 1863

When Johnnie comes marching home again
Hurrah! Hurrah!
We'll give him a hearty welcome then
Hurrah! Hurrah!
The men will cheer and the boys will shout
The ladies they will all turn out
And we'll all feel glad
When Johnnie comes marching home.

Note: This is a song from the American War Between the States (1861-1865). The song "the Ants Go Marching In" has the exact same tune.

Beginning Sounds

Lesson 49

Timed Activity (One Minute)

Blends

Instructor: *I am going to tell you a word. I want you to repeat the word – but I want you to leave out the ending two-letter blend.*

Example: If I say "fast" then you'd say, "fa"

Let's try two:

burst   bur

bolt   bo

Okay. Are you ready? Begin.

1. mast   ma
2. fact   fa
3. milk   mi
4. cold   co
5. clasp   cla
6. paint   pai
7. hoist   hoi
8. giant   gia
9. wrist   wri
10. blink   bli

Developing Expressive Language

Singing

Ten in the Bed
American Folk Song

There were ten in a bed and the little one said,

"Roll over, roll over" So they all rolled over and one fell out.

    There were nine in a bed and the little one said,

    "Roll over, roll over" So they all rolled over and one fell out.

There were eight in a bed and the little one said,

"Roll over, roll over" So they all rolled over and one fell out.

    There were seven in a bed and the little one said,

    "Roll over, roll over" So they all rolled over and one fell out.

There were six in a bed and the little one said,

"Roll over, roll over" So they all rolled over and one fell out.

    There were five in a bed and the little one said,

    "Roll over, roll over" So they all rolled over and one fell out.

There were four in a bed and the little one said,

"Roll over, roll over" So they all rolled over and one fell out.

    There were three in a bed and the little one said,

    "Roll over, roll over" So they all rolled over and one fell out.

There were two in a bed and the little one said,

"Roll over, roll over" So they all rolled over and one fell out.

    There was one in a bed and the little one said …. "I'm lonely"

Vowel Sounds

Lesson 50

Timed Activity

Instructor: *I am going to say a word. Then I want you to say the word sound of 'a, e, i, o and u.' For example, if I say "so" you should respond, 's' – the sound of the letter s and if I said "you", you should respond, 'y' – the sound of the letter y.*

Let's try two for practice:

    bee   (B)

    throw (Thr)

Okay. Are you ready? Begin.

1. ice   s
2. three   thr
3. open   pen
4. my   m
5. few   f
6. knee   kn
7. toe   t
8. eat   t
9. use   z
10. try   tr

Developing Expressive Language

Singing

Aiken Drum
(Scottish Folk Song)

There was a man lived in the moon, in the moon, in the moon.
There was a man lived in the moon and his name was Aiken Drum.

And he played upon a ladle, a ladle, a ladle.
He played upon a ladle and his name was Aiken Drum.

And his hair was made of spaghetti, spaghetti, spaghetti.
His hair was made of spaghetti and his name was Aiken Drum.

And his eyes were made of meatballs, meatballs, meatballs.
His eyes were made of meatballs and his name was Aiken Drum.

And he played upon a ladle, a ladle, a ladle.
He played upon a ladle and his name was Aiken Drum.

And his nose was made of cheese, cheese, cheese.
His nose was made of cheese and his name was Aiken Drum.

And his mouth was made of pizza, pizza, pizza.
His mouth was made of pizza and his name was Aiken Drum.

And he played upon a ladle, a ladle, a ladle.
He played upon a ladle and his name was Aiken Drum.

There was a man lived in the moon, in the moon, in the moon. There was a man lived in the moon and his name was Aiken Drum!

(Students could draw a picture of Aiken Drum.)

Vowel Sounds

Lesson 51

Timed Activity (One Minute)

Instructor: *I am going to say a word. Then, I want you to change the word by changing the sound of the vowel in the middle of the word. For example, if I say "feet" then you could correctly change that vowel long e sound to another vowel that makes a word;*

Feet can become Foot, Fit, Fate, fight, fat and so forth, lots of good choices. Try to quickly name at least two. Three are listed to show the instructor the concept.

Let's practice:

    bake: bike back book

    phone: fin fan fun

Okay. Are you ready? Begin.

1. Jake   joke, Jock, Jack
2. life   loaf, laugh, leaf
3. Sam   same, some, seem
4. lake   lock, lick, like
5. sass   sis, sauce, cease,
6. slip   slope, slop, slap
7. take   took, tyke, tick
8. track   trick, trike, truck
9. clock   click, cloak, cluck
10. song   sing, sang, sung

Developing Expressive Language

Singing

Crawdad Hole
(Southern Folk Music)

You get a line and I'll get a pole, Honey.
You get a line and I'll get a pole, Babe.
You get a line and I'll get a pole
And we'll go down to the crawdad hole,
Honey, Baby mine.

Whatcha' gonna' do when the creek goes dry, Honey?
Whatcha' gonna' do when the creek goes dry, Babe?
Whatcha' gonna' do when the creek goes dry?
Sit on the bank and cry, cry, cry,

Honey, Baby mine.

Beginning Sounds

Lesson 52

Timed Activity (One Minute)

Instructor: *I am going to say a word. I want you to change the beginning sound and make another word ... or two ... or three. Do it quickly so we can finish all of them. See just how many you can get.*

Example: I can say - toaster You could answer "roaster, coaster, poster"

Let's try one: many (penny, Denny, tinny, Jenny, Kenny.)

Okay. Are you ready? Begin.

1. tree   free three me
2. cat   fat bat gnat
3. toast   roast boast coast
4. drink   sink blink kink
5. sand   brand hand land
6. light   sight fight might
7. bike   Mike like hike
8. cone   bone, phone, lone

Note to the instructor: allow at least two seconds of no responses before moving to the next word.

Developing Expressive Language

Singing

Down by the Riverside
African American Folk Song

I'm gonna lay down my sword and shield
Down by the riverside
(Where?)
Down by the riverside.
(Where?)
Down by the riverside

I'm gonna lay down my sword and shield
Down by the riverside;
Ain't gonna study war no more!

Ain't gonna study war no more;
Ain't gonna study war no more;
Ain't gonna study war no more (no more!);
Ain't gonna study war no more;
Ain't gonna study war no more;
I ain't gonna study war no more.

I'm gonna shake hands around the world
Down by the riverside
(Where?)
Down by the riverside.
(Where?)
Down by the riverside

I'm gonna shake hands around the world
Down by the riverside;
Ain't gonna study war no more!

Ain't gonna study war no more;
Ain't gonna study war no more;
Ain't gonna study war no more (no more!);
Ain't gonna study war no more;
Ain't gonna study war no more;
I ain't gonna study war no more.

Ending Sounds

Lesson 53

Timed Activity (One Minute)

Instructor: *I am going to say a word. I want you to keep the very beginning sound of the word and then make new words.*

Example: If I say – truck - You could answer with any 'tr' word: "trick, trip, train"

Let's try a couple:

If I say – many - (market, More, Michael.)

If I say – jump – (juice, Jenny, giant)

Okay. Are you ready? Begin.

1. trunk   (true, trike, trim)   Answers are any "tr" word.
2. dirt   (dim, Dan, dice) Answers are any "d" word.
3. broom   (brick, brain, braces) … any "br" word.
4. fly   (fling, flow, flea) … any "fl" word.
5. tiger   (Tim, taste, tune) … any "t" word.
6. grape   (grab, granny, group) … any "gr" word.
7. buzz   (bite, bees, bike) … any "b" word.
8. drag   (drink, dry, drip) … any "dr" word.
9. chicken   (choose, chill, chase, chin) any "ch" word or "chi" word.
10. prince   (pretty, pro, praise) … any "pr" word.

Ending Sounds

Lesson 51

Activity (Untimed)

Instructions: *Ask each student to give their full name. Then ask for the ending sound of each name.*

Example: My name is Kenneth Urquhart Campbell. The last sound of Kenneth is "th" The ending sound for Urquhart is "t". The ending sound for Campbell is "l".

Instructions: *See if any of the students can make a rhyme from any one of their names to make another name.*

Example: My name is Ken. I can rhyme it with Ben or Finn.

Changing the Vowel Sounds

Lesson 54

Timed Activity (One Minute)

Instructor: *I am going to say a word. I want you to change the vowel sound and make another word ... or two ... or three. Do it quickly so we can finish all ten. See just how many you can get.*

Example: If I say - Mike, you could answer with words like meek or Mick)

Let's try a couple: cup   (cap, cape, keep)

                          green   (grain, groan, grin)

Okay. Are you ready? Begin.

1. file   (foal, full, fail)
2. sit   (sat, seat, set)
3. fire   (far, fur, four)
4. soap   (sip, sap, seep)
5. tip   (tap, top, tape)
6. mail   (mall, mole, mill)
7. bear   (boar, bur, buyer)
8. cake   (coke, crack, kick)
9. groan   (grain, green, grin)
10. sick   (sack, seek, psych)

Expressive Language Development

Singing

Apples and Bananas
(American Children's Song)

I like to eat, eat, eat   apples and bananas

I like to eat, eat, eat   apples and bananas

A lake to ate, ate, ate   ay-ples and ba-nay-nays

A lake to ate, ate, ate   ay-ples and ba-nay-nays

E leke to eat, eat, eat   ee-ples and bee-nee-nees

E leke to eat, eat, eat ee-ples and bee-nee-nees

I like to ite, ite, ite   i-ples and by-ny-nys

I like to ite, ite, ite i-ples and by-ny-nys

O loke to ote, ote, ote   oh-ples and bo-no-nos

O loke to ote, ote, ote oh-ples and bo-no-nos

U luke to oot, oot, oot   oo-ples and boo-noo-noos

U luke to oot, oot, oot oo-ples and boo-noo-noos

Section V

Morphemic Awareness and Language Acuity

Section V: Morphemic Awareness and Language Acuity

This section will prove to be quite difficult or impossible for many young children. In fact, adults have problems with doing some of these activities, especially those for whom English is their second language. If this section is too difficult, and this is easy to ascertain, do not proceed and thereby frustrate your students.

When we work with our children, we should make every effort to take them as far as we can while maintaining their motivation and generating successes. We must be careful not to ask for, nor demand, the impossible. At the same time we must take care not to limit the growth of our brightest students with low expectations. It is essential that as the work in phonological awareness becomes more difficult, your attitude remains upbeat and positive. The inability of a student to be successful in this section is no cause for alarm. If a child senses personal failure in one of these exercises, harm is being done. Again, keep your attitude upbeat and positive. Be prepared to move on to an activity in which they can have success. Once you sense the activity is too difficult or frustrating, it is time to move to something else.

If the lessons get to a point where they do not seem to be taking hold after the 2nd day, move on. If the activities move beyond the students' ability to grow, then consider the intervention complete. You are done.

Verb Tense

Lesson 55

Activity (Untimed)

Instructor: *I am going to say a word and then use a form of it in a sentence of what myself or someone else is doing right now. This is called the present. I want you to change the sentence to the past tense, changing it to mean the same thing happened yesterday or even last year.*

Let's try one. Race – I am racing to the store. Now, I will use the word race in the past tense.

*I **raced** to the store. Let's try one: Cook, as in I am cooking pie. Say it in the past tense. I cooked a pie.*

#	Verb	Sentence	Past
1.	eat	I am eating a sandwich.	ate
2.	play	He is playing with my friend.	played
3.	run	I am running in the park.	ran
4.	make	You are making cookies.	made
5.	throw	They are throwing the ball.	threw
6.	flip	She is flipping the pancakes.	flipped
7.	fall	He is falling down the mountain.	fell
8.	say	You are saying something silly.	said
9.	speak	They are speaking out loud.	spoke
10.	work	We are working in the shop.	worked

Verb Tense

Lesson 56

Activity (Untimed)

Instructor: *I am going to say a word that means I am doing something. Then, I am going to say a sentence that I want you to finish by changing the main word to the past tense.*

Let's try one. run   We run now, yesterday we _____.

bring I bring it now, yesterday I _____ it.

1.	mix	I mix now, yesterday I _____.	mixed
2.	make	I make it now, yesterday I _____ it.	made
3.	work	I work now, yesterday I _____.	worked
4.	drive	I drive now, yesterday I _____.	drove
5.	dig	I dig now, yesterday I _____.	dug
6.	kick	I kick now, yesterday I _____.	kicked
7.	fight	I fight now, yesterday I _____.	fought
8.	give	I give now, yesterday I _____.	gave
9.	toss	I toss now, yesterday I _____.	tossed
10.	fly	I fly now, yesterday I _____.	flew

Verb Tense

Lesson 57

Timed Activity (One Minute)

Instructor: *I am going to say a word that means I am doing something right now. Then, I am going to say a sentence that I want you to finish by changing the main action word to the past tense.*

Let's try one. tie   I tie my shoes today, yesterday I _____ my shoes.

sit   I sit down. Yesterday, I _____ down.

1.	sing	I sing today, yesterday I _____.	sang
2.	run	I run today, yesterday I _____.	ran
3.	climb	I climb today, yesterday I _____.	climbed
4.	think	I think today, yesterday I _____.	thought
5.	sleep	I sleep today, yesterday I _____.	slept
6.	buy	I buy today, yesterday I _____.	bought
7.	cook	I cook today, yesterday I _____.	cooked
8.	shoot	I shoot today, yesterday I_____.	shot
9.	swim	I swim today yesterday I_____.	swam
10.	float	I float today, yesterday I_____.	floated

Verb Tense

Lesson 58

Timed Activity (One Minute)

Instructor: *I am going to say a word that means I did something in the past, like yesterday or last year. We call that word a verb, meaning something happens, often with action. Then, I am going to say a sentence that I want you to finish or complete by changing the main verb to the present or right now tense.*

Let's try a few.

>*found – Yesterday, I found a quarter. I _____ lots of money on the ground.*

>*drank – I drank iced tea. Tomorrow mom said we will only have water to _____.*

1. felt   Yesterday I felt bad, today I _____ better.   (feel)

2. tried   Last week, I tried my best. Tomorrow I promise to _____ harder. (try)

3. sank   My friend built a boat and it sank. Mine did not _____. (sink)

4. wrote   I wrote a story. I love to _____.   (write)

5. flew   A bird flew off. The little bird is not yet ready to _____. (fly)

6. slept   This morning I slept in late. I really like to _____. (sleep)

7. sang   Yesterday, I sang with my little sister. My mother told me that we sound so nice when we _____. (sing)

8. swam   Last week it was warm so we swam. Right now it is too cold to _____. (swim)

9. kicked   I kicked the soccer ball into the net. The coach really likes the way I _____. (kick)

10. chewed   The meat was so tough I chewed and chewed. That meat is just too tough to _____. (chew)

Verb Tense

Lesson 59

Timed Activity
(One Minute)

Instructor: *I am going to say a word that means I did something in the past, like yesterday or last year. We call that word a verb, meaning something happens, often with action. Then, I am going to say a sentence that I want you to finish or complete by changing the main verb to the present or right now tense.*

Let's try a few. ate She ate too much chocolate. She really loves to eat.

drank – I drank grapefruit juice. My brother said grapefruit juice is too bitter for him to _____.

rang   1. I rang the doorbell twice. It appears it is broken and cannot _____. (ring)

tasted   2. I tasted the cookie dough ice cream. It was a wonderful to _____. (taste)

shut   3. Yesterday, I slammed the door shut so hard that I broke it and now it will not _____. (shut)

bought   4. I bought a beach ball with my allowance. I am old enough to ____ things on my own. (buy)

thought   5. I thought I would like licorice. Then, I tasted it. Now, I do not ____ I ever want to see the stuff again. (think)

believed   6. The little kid believed he could flap his arms fast enough to fly. That is impossible for me to _____. (believe)

caught   7. My Dad caught a cold. If I am not careful, I can _____ one too. (catch)

ate   8. I ate a double burger. Now, I am ready to _____ dessert. (eat)

cared   9. I cared for my neighbor's dog while they were on vacation. I did such a good job, they will pay me to _____ for the dog any time they are away. (care)

fell   10. She fell down the stairs. I have good balance, so I never _____. (fall)

Plurals

Lesson 60

Timed Activity (30 Seconds)

Instructor: *I am going to say a word that means one of something. If I say bird, I want you to change it to the word that means more than one bird; that is birds. Most often all we have to do is add the "s" sound. There are some words that we do not have to change to make it more than one, like deer or shrimp. There are others that really change, like the plural of mouse is mice.*

Let's try some.   One duck - Three ….. ducks

Here comes a trick one: One Fish …. Ten ….. Fish (Funny, we don't change that one.)

1. monkey ... (monkeys)
2. girl .... (girls)
3. lip .... (lips)
4. deer .... (deer)
5. country ... (countries)
6. box .... (boxes)
7. child .... (children)
8. mouse ..... (mice)
9. life .... (lives)
10. cap .... (caps)

Developing Expressive Language

Singing

There's a Hole
(Traditional Folk Song)

There's a hole in the middle of the sea
There's a hole in the middle of the sea
There's a hole, there's a hole. There's a hole in the middle of the sea

There's a log in the hole in the middle of the sea
There's a log in the hole in the middle of the sea
There's a log, there's a log, there's a log in the hole in the middle of the sea

There's a bump on the log in the hole in the middle of the sea
There's a bump on the log in the hole in the middle of the sea
There's a bump, there's a bum, there's a bump on the log in the hole in the middle of the sea

There's a frog on the bump on the log in the hole in the middle of the sea
There's a frog on the bump on the log In the hole in the middle of the sea
There's a frog, there's a frog, there's a frog on the bump on the log
in the hole in the middle of the sea

There's a fly on the frog on the bump on the log in the hole in the middle of the sea
There's a fly on the frog on the bump on the log in the hole in the middle of the sea
There's a fly, there's a fly, there's a fly on the frog on the bump on the log
in the hole in the middle of the sea

There's a wing on the fly on the frog on the bump on the log
In the hole in the middle of the sea
There's a wing on the fly on the frog on the bump
On the log in the hole in the middle of the sea
There's a wing, there's a wing, there's a wing on the fly on the frog
On the bum on the log in the hole in the middle of the sea

There's a flea on the wing on the fly on the frog on the bump
On the log in the hole in the middle of the sea
There's a flea on the wing on the fly on the frog on the bump on the log
In the hole in the middle of the sea
There's a flea, there's a flea, there's a flea on the wing on the fly
On the frog on the bump on the log
In the hole in the middle of the sea!!

Of course this song was written not only to drive the instructor completely nuts, but the entire class. But what a rapport builder these can be. And as you may guess, you can use your search engine and watch this entire song performed so that you can get the tune down before trying this with a class. What great fun!

Plurals

Lesson 61

Timed Activity (30 seconds)

Instructor: *I am going to say a word that means one of something. If I say bird, I want you to change it to the word that means more than one bird; that is birds. Most often all we have to do is add the "s" sound. There are some words that we do not have to change to make it more than one, like deer or shrimp. There are others that really change, like the plural of mouse is mice.*

Let's try some.   glass (glasses)

life   (lives)

Here comes a trick one: One fish …. Ten ….. fish (Funny, we don't have to change that one.)

1. man ...... (men)
2. woman .. (women)
3. girl .... (girls)
4. boy .... (boys)
5. foot .... (feet)
6. truck ..... (trucks)
7. fire .... (fires)
8. elf .... (elves)
9. calf .... (calves)
10. goose ... (geese)

Plurals

Lesson 62

Timed Activity (30 seconds)

Instructor: *I am going to say a word that means one of something. If I say bird, I want you to change it to the word that means more than one bird; that is birds. Most often all we have to do is add the "s" sound. There are some words that we do not have to change to make it more than one, like deer or shrimp. There are others that really change, like the plural of mouse is mice.*

Let's try some.   wife   (wives)

child   (children)

1. lizard .... (lizards)
2. person .... (people)
3. life .... (lives)
4. tree .... (trees)
5. sheep .... (sheep)
6. glass .... (glasses)
7. chef .... (chefs)
8. knife .... (knives)
9. roof .... (roofs)
10. key .... (keys)

Developing Expressive Language

Singing

Flying Purple People Eater
Sheb Wooley © 1958

This is a very fun song for little ones, especially the joke within the story that this monster only eats purple people – and there is no such thing. Get the song and the words from your search engine and have fun with this one. Children could have a lot of fun drawing and coloring a picture of the monster in this song.

It appears there is an art project in the description.

From Plural to Singular

Lesson 63

Timed Activity (30 seconds)

Instructor: *I am going to say a word that means several of something or more than one. If I say birds, I want you to change it to the word that means one, which is bird. Most often all we have to do is remove the "s" sound. There are times when we do something completely different.*

Let's try some.   birds   (bird)

lives   (life)

1. monkeys .... (monkey)
2. thieves .... (thief)
3. glasses .... (glass)
4. briefs .... (brief)
5. tries .... (try)
6. sheep .... (sheep)
7. oxen .... (ox)
8. bakeries .... (bakery)
9. children .... (child)
10. geese .... (goose)

Developing Expressive Language

Singing

There Was an Old Lady Who Swallowed a Fly
Tune written by Alan Mills and the lyrics by Rose Bonne © 1953

This song is one of those complex children's songs called a cumulative song. The line "perhaps she'll die" is often replaced by "I don't know why." Of course it is difficult and takes a class or child a number of times to master. But it is great fun, even to try to follow along and sing.

You can find many variations of great performances of this song over the years on the web.

Ordinal Numbers

Lesson 64

Activity (Untimed)

The student or class responds with the correct answer.

1. The winner comes in _____ place.   (first)

2. Right after the first one was number two. She came in _____. (second)

3. After that was number three. He came in _____.   (third)

4. The guy who came in number five came in _____ place. (fifth)

5. The kid who came in number nine came in _____ place.   (ninth)

6. A turtle came in last. He was number 100. We can say he came in last place or one _____ place.   (hundredth)

7. What place does the winner come in? (first)

8. What place does the very slowest person come in? (last)

9. When you think of number one, you think of _____ place. (first)

10. What birthday comes when the child turns four? _____ (fourth)

Developing Expressive Language

Ordinal Numbers

Activity 62

Line up the children. Then have them count off, "I'm first, I'm second, I'm third…'

Now everyone switch places with the shortest going first. Count off.

For the individual student, line up ten things on the table – it can be anything from black-eyed peas to pencils. Now, count them off, "First, second, third, forth, etc."

Have the student count them off.

Now point to various placements and have the student answer the place.

Language Facility and Morphology

Lesson 65 (Untimed)

Past Tense and Making Plurals

Instructor: *I am going to read you a sentence about one person doing something today. Then I want you to change the sentence so that there will be more than one person doing that same thing yesterday. We will not time this activity. We will do all six.*

(Note: There are many correct answer possibilities.)

Example: I am going to town today. (We went to town yesterday.)

You try one: He is playing basketball. (They were playing basketball.)

1. Sally is trying out to be a cheerleader. (Sally and her friends tried out to be cheerleaders. We tried out to be cheerleaders. They tried out to be cheerleaders.)

2. Bill is fishing. (Bill and his friends were fishing. We were fishing.)

3. My mom works every day. (My parents worked hard last year.. Mom and Dad worked last Sunday.)

4. That is very fun. (Those were very fun.)

5. Dad drives to work every day. (We drove to work yesterday.. We drove the car.

6. I am not very hungry. (We were not very hungry. My family was very hungry.)

Language Facility and Morphology

Working with Affixes

Preparing for Lesson 64

Words are made of parts. These parts have a root word or main part. The main part of the word telephone is phone. Prefixes and suffixes can be added to that root, as when we added the prefix "tele" to phone. We call these things that are added "affixes." When we add the plural affix 's' we get telephones.

The root can change according to time as in the use of past and present tense, for example, came and went. The root can also undergo a change when working with numbers, as in goose and geese. In English, prefixes, suffixes and root words often come from other languages and traditions, such as Latin, German and regional dialects. Thus, we have some of the rules of the other languages and traditions when we work with our words.

The lemma is a term that can be used for the root, stem or base word. For example the *lemma* (root word) of strawberries is berry. In effect we removed the "straw" and simplified to the singular "berries" to get berry, the lemma. The lemma of a verb would be the infinitive form of that verb without the word "to". Infinitives of common verbs are to eat, to sleep, to drink, to run, to jump, etc. The lemmas of the above infinitives are eat, sleep, drink, run, jump, etc. These lemmas can change to the words ate, slept, drank, jumped, etc. via verb tense changes.

Some lemmas never stand alone as in "ruth" which once meant compassion. Now, that lemma needs the affix "less" as in ruthless, meaning without compassion. Our students do not need to know these complexities; they will come naturally with their everyday use of the language. Knowing these formal terms help us understand the complexity in the manipulations of our language.

Working with Prefixes
Lesson 66 - Untimed

Open the lesson by defining these prefixes:

Re means again – like in replay or redo

Pre means before – like in preschool or preview

Un means not – like in untied or unglued

Mini means little – like in mini-golf or mini-skirt

Instructor: *I will say the word with the prefix. I will tell you what it means. Then, I want you to answer my question and then tell me a sentence with that word.*

1. Rewrite – *re* means "do it again – do what again? – The students say, "write again." Now use this in a sentence.

2. Preschool – *pre* means before – before what ?– before school or kindergarten . Now use it is a sentence.

3. Unhappy – *un* means not – not what?– not happy

4. Nonsense – *non* means not – not what ?– not making sense

5. Unbelievable– *un* means not – not what – not believable

6. Redo – *re* means again – again what? – do again

Note to the Instructor: This concept may prove challenging to some students and may require more practice. You can show with many examples that sometimes by knowing what the prefix is, you may be able to figure out what the word means. Preview, for example, means before you view or before you see.

Working with Prefixes

Lesson 67 - Untimed

Open the lesson by defining these prefixes:

Dis means not – like discomfort or disconnect

Mini means little – minivan or minicam

Non means not – like nonsense or nonstick

Re means again – like re-elect or redo

1. Disappear – *dis* means not – not what? – not appear
2. Miniskirt – *mini* means little – little what? – little skirt
3. Nonstick – *non* means not – not what? – not stick
4. Replay – *re* means again – again what? – play again
5. Disagree – *dis* means not – not what? – not agree
6. Nonliving - *non* means not – not what? - not living

Working with Prefixes

Lesson 68 - Untimed

Working with Prefixes

Instructor: *I am going to give you a prefix and define it for you. I then want you to name as many words as you can that contain that prefix.*

1. *Re* is a prefix meaning to do it again – name 3 words that use the prefix "re"
   rerun redo replay retell replace

2. *Pre* is a prefix meaning before – name 3 words that use the prefix "pre".

   preview pretend prepay pregame prepare precook

3. *Un* is a prefix meaning not – un words?

   unbelievable, unreal, undo, unexpected, unusual

4. *Non* is a prefix also meaning not – non words?

   nonstick nonsense nonstop nonreader nonbeliever

5. *Dis* is a prefix that also means not

   disabled disappear disagree discount dislocated

Working with Prefixes

Lesson 69 - Untimed

Working with Prefixes

Instructor: *I am going to give you a prefix and define it for you. I then want you to name as many words as you can that contain that prefix.*

1. *Tele* is a prefix meaning across – name 3 tele words.

    telescope television telephone telegraph

2. *Mini* is a prefix meaning small – name 3 mini words

    miniskirt minimal minivan minicam

3. *De* is a prefix meaning opposite – name 3 de words.

    detour derail debug debone destruct

4. *Anti* is a prefix meaning opposite or against – name 3 anti words.

    anitfreeze antibiotics antiwar antivenom

5. *Mis* is a prefix meaning wrong or a mistake – name 3 mis words.

    misdirect misuse mistake miscalculate misunderstand

Working with Prefixes

Lesson 70 - Untimed

Review these prefixes with the students.

mis means bad	sub means under	fore means in front
trans means across	anti means against	mid means middle
re means again	semi means half	over means too much

Directions: *I am going to read you a word. Then I will tell you the prefix, what it means. Then I want you to tell me a sentence with the word in it.*

1. Misspell – the prefix mis means bad – bad what? bad spelling – or to spell incorrectly.

2. Submarine - the prefix *sub* means – under – under what? - under marine or under water – or a ship that travels underwater

3. Forehead means - in front – the front of the head

4. Transport means across and carry – carry across – to move something

5. Antifreeze means against turn to ice – antifreeze – against freezing

6. Midlife – mid means middle – the middle of life

7. Remake – remake means make again

8. Semicircle- means half of a circle

9. Overeat – means to eat too much

10. Antiwar – anti means agains – against what? against war.

Expressive Language

Activity 71 - Untimed

Working with Prefixes

Review these prefixes with the students.

mis means bad	*sub means under*	*fore means in front*
trans means across	*anti means against*	*mid means middle*
re means again	*semi means half*	*over means too much*

1. *Mis* is a prefix meaning bad – give me two mis words
    (mistake mismatch misbehave)
2. *Sub* is a prefix meaning under – give me two sub words
    (submarine subway subterranean)
3. *Fore* is a prefix meaning in front – give me two fore words
    (forehead forewarn forward)
4. *Trans* is a prefix meaning across – give me two trans words
    (transport transatlantic transfer)
5. *Anti* is a prefix meaning against – give me two anti words
    (antibiotics antifungal antiaircraft)
6. *Mid* is a prefix meaning middle – give me two mid words
    (midway midwest midsummer)
7. *Re* is a prefix meaning again – give me two re words
    (return rerun redo)
8. *Semi* is a prefix meaning half – give me two semi words
    (semitruck semicircle semiretired)

Working with Suffixes

Lesson 72 - Untimed

Working with - ing

Instructor: *We can change words by adding endings to them. I can take a verb like swim and by adding an ing to the end change it to swimming. I can swim; I am swimming. I can take the word play and change it to playing. I can play; I am playing.*

I am going to give you a word; then I want you to put an –ing on the ending and then tell me a sentence. For example, if I say dream, you would say dreaming, then something like "I am dreaming of Christmas."

Let's do one for practice – eat …

Okay, let's begin.

1. change
2. throw
3. fly
4. run
5. drive
6. chase
7. call
8. erase
9. surf
10. race

Working with Suffixes

Lesson 73 - Untimed

Working with - er

Instructor: *We can change words by adding endings to them. I can take a verb like swim and by adding an er to the end change it to swimmer. I can swim; I am a swimmer. I can take the word play and change it to player. I can play; I am a player.*

I am going to give you a word; then I want you to put an -er on the ending. Then tell me a sentence with that word. For example, if I say dream, you would say dreamer, then something like "They say she is a dreamer."

Let's do one for practice – bake… (baker)

Okay, let's begin.

1. farm
2. teach
3. work
4. paint
5. sting
6. drive
7. hop
8. train
9. kick
10. pitch

Developing Expressive Language
Singing
Kookaburra
Written by Marion Sinclair. ©1932 Larrikin Publishing Pty Ltd.

Kookaburra is a wonderful song that will give your child or children a feel for Australia and you an excellent opportunity to teach a bit about "the Land Down Under."

You can show your class the song and tune by finding it on your search engine.

This is also another drawing opportunity.

Working with Suffixes

Lesson 74 - Untimed

Working with -tion and -sion

Instructor: *We can change words by adding endings to them. I can take a verb like celebrate and by adding a tion to the end, change it to the noun celebration. Examples: I can celebrate. After winning I will go to the celebration. I can add numbers in my head. What I am doing is called addition.*

I am going to give you a word; then I want you to put a –tion/sion on the ending and see if you can come up with the word. Sometimes you have to change it a little bit. Then, give me a sentence with the new word we have made. For example, if I say subtract, you would say subtraction, and then give me a sentence like, "We were working with subtraction in math."

Let's do one for practice – operate …(operation)

Okay, let's begin.

1. confess .... (confession)
2. elect .... (election)
3. react .... (reaction)
4. act .... (action)
5. discuss .... (discussion)
6. graduate .... (graduation)

Working with Suffixes

Lesson 75 - Untimed

Working with – *ician*

Instructor: *I am going to give you a word; then I want you to put an –ician, (pronounced ish-un) on the ending and then tell me the new word and use it in a sentence The suffix –ician means "someone who does". For example, if I say music, you would say musician, then something like "My sister is a rock musician."*

Let's do one for practice – magic …

Okay, let's begin.

1. politics .... (politician)
2. beauty .... (beautician)
3. music   .... (musician)
4. pediatric .... (pediatrician)
5. electric .... (electrician)
6. magic .... (magician)

Introducing Comparatives and Superlatives

We can change words by adding endings to them. I can take a word that describes something – an adjective – and have it also work for two and even more things.

Okay, let's begin. We add an 'er for when we are talking about comparing two and we add an 'est' for when we are comparing more than two things.

Hungry – I am hungrier than you. I am the hungriest of all.

So, for two people, I am hungrier. When it involves more than two, it is hungriest.

Fast – I am faster than you. I am the fastest of all.

Comparatives/Superlatives

Lesson 76

Exercise

Instructor: *Now, lets see how many we can get in a minute. I will tell you the word, then I will begin a sentence, you will tell me without raising your hand what word belongs in the sentence. Ready? Begin.*

1. old – Of the two of us, I am the _____ one. *older*

2. fast – I am the _____ runner in the class. *Fastest*

3. slow – Between a turtle and a snail, which is _____? *slower*

4. nice – My teacher is the _____ one in the school. *nicest*

5. rich – She is _____ than her sister. *richer*

6. poor – Haiti is one of the _____ countries in the world. *poorest*

7. happy – Is it true that poor people are the _____ in the world. *happiest*

8. sad – Who is _____, a clown or a juggler? *sadder*

9. funny – Who is _____, a clown or a juggler? *funnier*

10. smart – I am the _____ person in the class. *smartest*

Reversing Words

Lesson 77 - Untimed

Instructor: *I am going to carefully say a word. I want you to listen and then tell me what it would sound like if you said the word backwards, the last sound first and the first sound last. Thinking backwards is not an easy thing to do.*

If I say sun you would say, "nus".

If I say bake, you would say, "Kabe"

You try a couple Bike (Kibe)   Ache (Kay)

1. dime .... (mide)
2. bet .... (teb)
3. eat .... (tee)
4. pay .... (ape)
5. pass .... (sap)
6. phone .... (nofe)
7. boy .... (oib)
8. sat .... (tas)
9. pain .... (nape)
10. shoe .... (oosh)

This is a high level skill of phonemic awareness. I tell the student a word and their job is to reverse it. Cat become tack. Ken become Neck. Lip becomes pill. Me becomes eem.

Can you say your name backwards? We may first need to write it down. This is easiest to do with a nickname.

215

Preparing to work with
Spoonerisms

Poor old Dr. Archibald Spooner; he had this very embarrassing habit of switching parts of words around in ways that made what he was supposed to be saying into something often quite silly.

For instance, instead of saying, "healing the sick", he would say, "sealing the hick." Instead of saying, "We need to light a fire," he would say, "We need to fight a liar."

This is a guessing game. We will not need a timer. It should be fun trying to figure out what is meant from what has been said. When you understand how Spoonerisms work, you can make them up yourself. Be on the look out for when someone speaking messes up and says a Spoonerism.

Spoonerisms

Lesson 78 (Untimed)

Spooneristic Food

Tell the students the Dr. Spooner story. Then begin the activity.

Instructor: *I am going to mess up a food like Dr. Spooner would a long, long time ago. Your job is to figure out the food I am talking about. I will do the Spoonerism, raise your hand when you can figure out what I'm meaning to say.*

1. sticken chrips .... (chicken strips)
2. wicken chings .... (chicken wings)
3. wuffalo bings .... (Buffalo wings)
4. Pill dickles .... (dill pickles)
5. can pakes .... (pancakes)
6. mookies and kilk .... (cookies and milk)
7. chickolate cop chookies .... (chocolate chip cookies)
8. chilled greaze................... (grilled cheese)
9. stilly feeze chake .... (Philly Cheesesteak)
10. bamdurger .... (hamburger)
11. dot hawg .... (hot dog)
12. peez cheetza .... (cheese pizza)
13. chopata pips .... (potato chips)
14. sops pickle .... (Popsicle)
15. chish and fipps................. (fish and chips)
16. nelly joduts....................... (jelly donuts)
17. knee butt putter .... (peanut butter)
18. trench foast .... (French toast)
19. sam hand witch................ (ham sandwich)
20. palt and sepper .... (salt and pepper)

Spoonerisms

Lesson 79

Spooneristic Creatures

1. bumming herd .... hummingbird
2. Petland shoney .... Shetland pony
3. Manish spackerel .... Spanish mackeral
4. fellyjish .... jellyfish
5. duel bog .... bulldog
6. patter killer .... caterpillar
7. rock croach .... cockroach
8. Dock O'Crial .... crocodile
9. full brog .... bullfrog
10. Gilly boat .... billygoat
11. fed rocks .... red fox
12. key pock .... peacock
13. runny babbit .... bunny rabbit
14. snattle rake .... rattlesnake
15. Dane rear .... reindeer
16. he source .... seahorse
17. weight shite gark .... great white shark
18. ring stay .... stingray
19. tapping snurtle .... snapping turtle
20. pood wecker .... woodpecker

Spoonerisms

Lesson 80 (Untimed)

Spooneristic Things

1. led right .... redlight
2. terry fail .... fairy tale
3. mopping shawl .... shopping mall
4. posh hittel .... hospital
5. bain row .... rainbow
6. bokker Saul .... soccer ball
7. stuss bop .... bus stop
8. no tell .... toenail
9. shase spip......................... spaceship
10. bow coy............................ cowboy
11. dargen.............................. garden
12. burf sword .... surf board
13. why hay............................ highway
14. foons and sporks.............. spoons and forks
15. kohler roaster .... roller coaster
16. cumper bars .... bumper cars
17. a ripe tighter .... typewriter
18. free ridge aerator .... refrigerator
19. a boat nook .... a notebook
20. a bite lulb .... a light bulb

219

Spoonerisms

Lesson 81 (Untimed)

Spooneristic Places

1. You nork .... New York
2. Falli Cornia .... California
3. Keximo .... Mexico
4. Rare Toe Peeko .... Puerto Rico
5. Well a dare .... Delaware
6. Stack a pan .... Pakistan
7. Wally Hood .... Hollywood
8. Sansas Kitty .... Kansas City
9. Wee Kest .... Key West
10. Keeter .... Turkey
11. Jail bum .... Belgium
12. Late Grakes .... Great Lakes
13. Tin Kucky .... Kentucky
14. Sennity .... Tennessee
15. Lana Hoo Hoo .... Honolulu
16. my yack bard .... my back yard
17. the sack beat .... the back seat
18. Stankee Yadium .... Yankee Stadium
19. Chass uh Moose Its .... Massachusetts
20. Danakuh .... Canada

220

Spoonerisms

Lesson 82 (Untimed)

Instructor: *I am going to say a sentence just like I was old Dr. Spooner. I want you to see if you can figure out what I meant. (These are not perfect phoneme switches).*

1. Look, in the yard, I see a **runny babbit!**
2. We just bought a new **veletision.**
3. When my parents go out, they hire a **sabie bitter.**
4. I need an umbrella. It is **roaring pain.**
5. Tell me the story about the **pea little thrigs.**
6. My spaceship can travel the **leed of spight.**
7. Dad, you can come in now. I'm **shout of the hour.**
8. I went to the candy store to buy some **belly jeans.**
9. I hit my **bunny phone** on the desk. Ouch!
10. My mother is painting her **no tails.**
11. I have a cold and need to **know my blows.**
12. *I see a* **flutterby flitting** *on the* **sower**.
13. Before the children can go out to play, they must all **chew their doors.**
14. My **stickers** are all **fingy.**
15. I saw a **snattle rake** in the grass.
16. **Rindercella slopped** her **glass dripper.**
17. I live just a bit off of **strain meat.**
18. I watch **Taturday Corning Martoons.**
19. The happy man is **ringing** in the **Seine.**
20. One, two – **shuckle** my **boo!**

Listening Acuity

Lesson 83 - Untimed

Language Acuity – Acuity in Standard English

Instructor: *I am going to say a sentence. Something in the sentence will not make sense or be incorrect. I want you to say the sentence correctly. Let's do a few for practice.*

I ate five piece of candy.   *(I ate five pieces of candy.)*

They is coming to town.   *(They are coming to town.)*

You go with me?   *(Will you go with me?)*

Let's begin.

1. I am the better of all.   (I am the best of all.)

2. I want an order of French fry.   (I want an order of French fries.)

3. I will sit in the front seats of the car with Dad. (I will sit in the front seat of the car with Dad.)

4. School start tomorrow.   (School starts tomorrow.)

5. I had a scary dreams last night.   (I had a scary dream last night. I had scary dreams last night.)

6. They is so much fun to be with.   (They are so much fun to be with.)

7. I will came with you.   (I will come with you.)

8. Seven creepy spider on the wall.   (Seven creepy spiders are on the wall, were on the wall, etc.)

9. Look down at the sky.   (Look up at the sky.)

10. I want to go skating at the pool.   (I want to go swimming at the pool; or I want to go skating at the rink.)

Language Acuity

Lesson 84 - Untimed

Instructor: *I will tell you a sentence. It is incorrect. Often, there will be more than one thing wrong with it. Parts of it may not even make good sense. I want you to correct it for me.*

1. **My brother be hungry.** — My brother is hungry.

2. **Three truck crashed.** — Three trucks crashed.

3. **They is so silly.** — They are so silly.

4. **I am best than my sister.** — I am better than my sister.

5. **Who makes the better pizza in the whole world?** — Who makes the best pizza in the whole world.

6. **I want a bowl of soups for lunch.** — I want a bowl of soup for lunch. I want two bowls of soup for lunch.

7. **It is rain outside.** — It is raining outside. It is rainy outside.

8. **I am run real fast.** — I am running real fast. I am running really fast. I

9. **It is very hot. Maybe it will snows.** — It is very cold. Maybe it will snow.

10. **My grandmother is fifteen years old.** — (change number or change subject)

Language Acuity

Lesson 85 - Untimed

Instructor: I will tell you a sentence. It is incorrect. Often, there will be more than one thing wrong with it. Parts of it may not even make good sense. I want you to correct it for me.

1. **Him is going fishing with she.** ....(He is going fishing with her.)

2. **Me don't wants no hot dog.**..................(I do not want a hot dog.)

3. **Them is coming over to play.**................(They are coming over to play.)

4. **I don't wants nothing.**...........................(I don't want anything.)

5. **When is me turn?**.................................(When is my turn?)

6. **That is she's purse.** ....(That is her purse.)

7. **Them is having great fun.** ....(They are having great fun.)

8. **Him is my father.**..................................(He is my father.)

9. **Her is my mother.** ....(She is my mother.)

10. **That is him's ball.**...............................(That is his ball.)

Language Acuity

Lesson 86 - Untimed

Instructor: *I will tell you a sentence. It is incorrect. Often, there will be more than one thing wrong with it. Parts of it may not even make good sense. I want you to correct it for me.*

1. **Him are not real funny.** .... (He is not real funny)

2. **John are the bigger one of all.** .... (John is the biggest one of all.)

3. **Me sure is hungry.** .... (I sure am hungry.)

4. **Carol am go to get she ball.** .... (Carol is going to get her ball.)

5. **Mason make him sandwich.** .... (Mason makes his sandwich.)

6. **How me going to buy she candy?** ...... (How am I going to buy her candy?)

7. **Them boys is coming with us.** .... (Those boys are coming with us.)

8. **Him are the taller boy in the class.** ..... (He is the tallest boy in the class.)

9. **Can us goes with you?** .... (Can we go with you?)

10. **Why are him so fastest?** .... (Why is he so fast?)

Note: There are a number of acceptable responses.

Logic (Conditionals)

Lesson 87

Instructor: *Please complete these sentences with answers that make good sense. See if you can get more than one answer for each.*

Example: When I play very hard, then _____. I get tired. I get dirty. I turn red in the face. I get thirsty.

1. If I am hungry, then ___.
2. What goes up must come _____.
3. If I work really hard, then _____.
4. When I am tired, then _____.
5. If I get up too early, then _____.
6. When I see monkeys flying, then _____.
7. If I am going to the movies then I need _____.
8. If I see my sister then _____.
9. If I play in the rain then _____.
10. If you come over to my house then _____.

We are working here to develop and reinforce thinking out from what are fairly open-ended prompts. Not only are there multiple correct responses, multiple responses should be encouraged. Those taking the prompt the extra mile need special encouragement.

Developing Expressive Language
Singing
Oh Susannah
Stephen Foster - 1848

I come from Alabama with a banjo on my knee.

I'm going to Louisiana, my true love for to see.

It rained all night the day I left, the weather it was dry.

The sun so hot, I froze to death.   Susannah, don't you cry.

    Oh, Susannah, Oh don't you cry for me;

    for I come from Alabama with a banjo on my knee.

I had a dream the other night, when everything was still.

I dreamed I saw Susannah dear, a-coming down the hill.

The buckwheat cake was in her mouth,

the tear was in her eye.

I said, "I'm coming from the south,

Susannah, don't you cry."

    Oh, Susannah, Oh don't you cry for me.

        For I come from Alabama with a banjo on my knee.

Section VI

Apendix

Appendix

Scope and Sequence

Sound Awareness

Simple Word and Pseudo-word Repeating – Lessons 1,2,3

Working with Pseudo Words – Lesson 4

Simple Sentence Repeating – Lessons 5,6,7,8

Identification of words by tapping – Lessons 9,10,11

Making words from Syllables – Lesson 12

Finding Syllables from Words – Lesson 13

Defining Meaning of Words or Phrases – Lessons 14, 16,17,18

Making sentences from Words or Phrases – Lessons 14,19,20

Rhyming – Lessons 21,22,23,24,25,26,27,28,29,30,31,32

Phonemic Awareness

Working with Phonemes (Beginning Sounds) – 31,33,34,40,41,42,43,50

Working with Phonemes (Ending Sounds) – 32,38,44,46,51

Working with Phonemes (Alliteration) – 35,36

Working with Phonemes (Blends) – 37,45,47

Working with Phonemes (Using Contextual Clues) – 39

Working with Phonemes (Vowel Sounds) – 48,49,52

Advanced Sound Manipulation (Reversals) – 75

Advanced Sound Manipulation (Spoonerisms) – 76,77,78,79,80

Morphological Awareness

Verb Tense (Present to Past) – 53,53,55

Verb Tense (Past to Present) – 56,57

Singular to Plural – 58,59,60

Plural to Singular – 61

Prefixes – 64,65,66,67,68,69

Suffixes – 70,71,72,73,74

Comparatives and Superlatives – 74

Language Awareness

Ordinal Awareness - 62

Language Facility – 63,64

Language Acuity – 81,82,83,84

Logic – Conditionals - 85

Song List

Hey Mickey

Where Are You Tonight?

Mommy Loves Me

Hit the Road Jack

Have You Ever Seen a Lassie

My Bonnie

For He's a Jolly Good Fellow

Skinny Marink

The Itsy Bitsy Spider

My Hands on My Head

Brother John (Frère Jacques)

One, Two Buckle My Shoe

The Hokey Pokey

Here We Go Round the Mulberry Bush

Shoo Fly

Joy to the World

The Bear Went Over the Mountain

Dem Bones

The Little Green Frog

If You're Happy and You Know It

I'm a Little Teapot

Hey, Ho Nobody Home

Take Me Out to the Ballgame

I'm Henery the Eighth

Knick Knack

Miss Mary Mack

It's Raining

Pop Goes the Weasel

Over the River and Through the Woods

Cinderella Dressed in Yella

The Ants Go Marching

I've Been Working on the Railroad

If I Had a Hammer

A Sailor Went to Sea

Tiny Tim the Turtle

Billy Goat Hide and Seek

Engine, Engine Number Nine

Suwanee River (Old Folks at Home)

She Threw It Out the Window

The Muffin Man

Yankee Doodle

John Jacob Jingleheimer Schmidt

The Grand Old Duke of York

This Little Light of Mine

Little Liza Jane

Clementine

When Johnny Comes Marching Home

Ten in the Bed

Aiken Drum

You Get a Line (Crawdad Hole)

Down by the Riverside

Apples and Bananas

There's a Hole

Flying Purple People Eater

There Was an Old Lady Who Swallowed a Fly

Kookaburra

Oh, Susannah

Great Leaps and RTI (Response to Intervention)

Great Leaps has been designed to accommodate a wide variety of student need. This flexibility allows *Great Leaps* to be a program available for all three levels of RTI.

Tier 1: At Tier 1 students receive instruction within an evidence-based, scientifically researched core program. Usually, the Tier 1 instructional program is synonymous with the core reading or math curriculum that is typically aligned with state standards. The intent of the core program is the delivery of a high-quality instructional program in reading or math that has established known outcomes that cut across the skill development of the targeted area. All 5 and six year old children should be screened in phonemic-phonological and language awareness skills. A daily group intervention with an observant instructor using *Great Leaps Phonological Awareness and Language Development Activities for the Emergent Reader* (evidence-based practices using well researched tactics and interventions) can be of great assistance in the process of determining which children gain from the regular classroom instruction as well as those having difficulties.

Students who appear to be having significant difficulties with little or no daily progress should first be moved to five minutes a day of more individualized *Great Leaps* while a referral for assessment and more intensive intervention proceeds. If there is a group of children having similar difficulties, a small group placement would suffice. Early intervention, especially in children with dyslexia or traumatic brain injury, is so critical that professional diagnosis should begin post haste. Early placement and treatment in many cases considerable lessens the need for services later.

Tier Two: This level of instruction would involve a professional trained in remediating and helping students with possible disabilities whose response in the regular teaching environment has been inadequate. It may involve taking the student of her regular class for a portion of the day. Early childhood education interventions could involve a brief pullout with *Great Leaps* for a smaller group of students with intensified and more personalized instruction. The professional involved with these students should be adept at the referral process as well as communicating the academic and social performance of the students to the assessment and placement professionals.

Tier 3: Many students in tier 3 settings require a daily systematic intervention in reading and language acquisition, very often one on one. Great Leaps is organized so as to help these students move step at a time to the mastery of phonological and phonemic awareness. The professionals involved in these classrooms and interventions must have the skills to make considerable adjustments to the pace and execution of the program to meet the requirements of the individual goals of each student. These professionals must also be adept at gauging student potential and developing the plan to achieve it. *Great Leaps* has been designed to easily accommodate many of these students in an efficient, motivating set of activities that are relatively simple to implement with fidelity.

Glossary

Affixes – the sound or letters that can be added to words to alter or further clarify their meanings. Usually this refers to prefixes and suffixes.

Alliteration - the repetition of a particular sound, most often the beginning sound, in a series of words or phrases. Example: Sally sang a song.

Automaticity - the ability to perform a skill without mental processing. It is usually achieved as the result of learning, repetition, and practice.

Comparatives - adding an *'er'* to an adjective or adverb to compare it against a noun or verb. Example: I am taller than a turtle. I run faster than you.

Conditionals – an if-then statement is a conditional. Example: If it is cloudy, it may rain.

Consonant Blends - groups of two or three consonants in words that make a distinct consonant sound, such as "bl" or "spl."

Contextual or Context Clues - hints within a reading selection that the author has given to help define a difficult or new term. Example: We shivered as the *frigid* weather moved in from the north. The words *north* and *shivered* suggest to us that frigid means cold.

Digital Countdown Timer – an electronic timer that can be set to a certain amount of time and display the countdown as the allotted time passes.

Emergent Readers - students that are just beginning to grasp the basic concepts of book and print.

Equal Ratio Chart – a multiply-divide chart that shows movement in percentages as opposed to equal intervals.

Expressive Language – verbal language

Gerunds - nouns formed from a verb by adding '*-ing*'. In "to teach", learn is a verb. Teaching becomes a noun as in, "Teaching is a profession"

Immediate Correction – whenever an error is made, correction and modeling within a second or so of the miscue

Language Acuity – the ability to know the sound of the language so well as to be able to easily pick out errors of sense and grammar

Language Experience – the use of a student's existing language skills to further reading, writing and comprehension skills

Language Facility – ease with the language

Lemma - a term that can be used for the root, stem or base word.

Mastery – the complete and lasting understanding of a concept

Modeling – directly showing a student how something is to be done.

Morphologic Awareness - the recognition, understanding, and use of the parts of words that carry significance. For example, root words, prefixes, suffixes, and grammatical inflections are all morphemes which can be added or taken away from a word to alter its meaning.

Morphemes - the smallest semantic units in a language. Every word comprises one or more morphemes.

Mother Goose - the imaginary author of a collection of English fairy tales and nursery rhymes

Oral Expression - coherent, verbal speech

Ordinal Numbers - the words representing the rank of a number with respect to some order, in particular order or position (i.e., *first*, *second*, *third*, etc.).

Phonemic awareness - a subset of phonological awareness in which listeners are able to hear, identify and manipulate phonemes.

Phonemes - the smallest segmental units of sound employed

Phonological or Sound Awareness - the detection and manipulation of sounds at three levels: (1) syllables, (2) onsets and rimes, and (3) phonemes.

Phonics - the method for teaching reading and writing the English language by developing learners' phonemic awareness in order to teach the correspondence between sounds and the spelling patterns these sounds represent.

Plurals – word forms in nouns that indicate more than one.

Prefix - affixes which are placed before the root of a word.

Proficiency – basic competence and understanding of a skill.

Pseudo-words – words that have absolutely no meaning

Receptive Language - the process involved in the understanding of the spoken word.

Response to Intervention (RTI) - a method of academic intervention required in the United States to provide early, systematic assistance to children who are having learning problems.

Rhyme - a repetition of similar sounds in two or more words most often seen in poetry and songs. In the specific sense, two words rhyme if their final stressed vowel and all following sounds are identical.

Rime – that which can be similar in sound, especially with respect to the last syllable

Scope and Sequence - refers to the breadth and depth of a specific curriculum. For instance, the scope is how much you are going to teach of a subject over the course of a semester or year. The sequence is the order and indication in which the lessons are presented.

Spoonerism - an error in speech or deliberate play on words in which corresponding consonants, vowels, or morphemes are switched. It is named after the Reverend William Archibald Spooner (1844–1930), Warden of New College, Oxford, who was notoriously prone to this tendency. The ability to translate a spoonerism is a sign of advanced phonological (sound) awareness.

Suffixes (postfixes or endings) - affixes that are placed after the stem of words to change or further define their meanings.

Superlatives – affixes that are placed after the stem of words to indicate the most or least of something. *Example: She is the fastest runner in the world.*

Syllabication – the breaking of a word into its syllables. Example: raccoon divided into syllables is *rac-coon.*

Syllable - one or more letters representing a single, uninterrupted sound.

Verb Tense - the form of a verb that indicates the time involved, be it past, present, future, etc. The tense can also indicate whether the action is ongoing or complete.

Vowels - the letters a, e, i, o and u. When the letter y has a long e sound, as in lonely, it is a vowel.